D1546317

Combat and Campus: Writing Through War

"Sgt. Peter Langlois and his sister, Annette Langlois Grunseth, reveal a priceless treasure in these pages. There is no better way to understand how the Vietnam War impacted an entire generation than to read these eloquent letters and poems. As witnesses to the effects of war at home, on a U.S. college campus, and in Vietnam, in the heat of combat, they lead us to understand how the war continues to reverberate in our hearts and lives."

— Ruth W. Crocker, author of *Those Who Remain: Remembrance and Reunion After War*

Combat and Campus: Writing Through War fulfills the promise Annette Langlois Grunseth made to her mother, that she will find a way to publish the letters her brother Peter wrote home from Vietnam. Peter Langlois had been drafted fresh out of college and soon deployed to an area of fierce fighting near the Cambodian border. He wrote war-seared letters with the precision of the journalist he studied to be: rice paddy, rubber plantation, ambush, bomb and artillery craters, medevacs. Bodies. Body parts. Peter's letters and Grunseth's tough-minded and tender poems tell the story of multiple levels of courage, urging us, hope against hope, never to go again to war.

— Margaret Rozga, author of *Holding My Selves Together,* 2019-2020 Wisconsin Poet Laureate

Poet Annette Langlois Grunseth has gathered her brother's eye-witness letters from the Vietnam War some fifty years ago, bringing us home-ground truth about those divisive times. Sgt. Peter R. Langlois's letters eloquently spell out war's tedium and horror. In her own poems thinking back, his sister's poems count the cost, then and on return to civilian life. It's a riveting, heart-breaking, read, and I couldn't put it down.

— Robin Chapman, poet, author of *The Only Home We Know*
(Tebot Bach)

Losing a brother or sister is a special brand of heartache, but Annette Grunseth has turned that heartache into a triumphant book. The interplay of her poetry and her brother's letters home as a soldier in Vietnam in *Combat and Campus: Writing Through War* is intimate, nuanced and compelling. It doesn't hurt that both sister and brother can write their marled socks off. Sgt. Peter Langlois' insights from the front lines are a revelation to me, and although I was privileged to read many of Annette's poems in draft, reading her poems of childhood, the turbulent 60's, and the aftermath of war in a context of love and anxiety for her brother adds poignant dimension. Annie Lamott has famously said, "We forget so much." Yet Annette's book is not only a fully realized tribute to her brother, it is an urgent reminder of events we shouldn't neglect, so that they can continue to inform our future.

— Tori Grant Welhouse, poet, author of prize-winning
YA novel, *The Fergus*

Combat and Campus: Writing Through War is a moving, respectful, and honest book that accurately recalls the days of conflict in Vietnam and at home. This book has stayed with me, reawakening memories for those of us who lived through the war. For newer generations, this book should be required reading in classrooms across the country. There is nothing I know like this; it is beautifully balanced between war and home, combat and campus, prose and poetry. It is an unputdownable account of our nation's trauma, encapsulated in the experience of one family.

— Judith Heide Gilliland, author of *The Day of Ahmed's Secret*
and *Strange Birds*

There is a powerful, historically accurate story in this book that Annette Langlois Grunseth has put together from her own poetry and letters from her brother's Vietnam experience. The story starts in childhood, moves on to her brother's experiences in boot camp, moves to harrowing, graphic experiences in some of the most difficult fighting in Vietnam, and ends in the denouement of poetry and loss. Peter Langlois did not die in Vietnam, but the loss from the war, documented in the letters he wrote, haunted his life and still haunts his family's life all these years later. History is important because it defines who we have been as we evolve into who we are and will be. Poetry is important because it explores the spiritual substance of who we have been, who we are and will be. This book acts as both primary source history and a poetic exploration of what Vietnam meant to one family and the nation both yesterday and on into the contemporary world. It is an important book that helps define some of the whirlpools that American society has inherited from the past.

— Thomas Davis, novelist, historian, poet, author of
In the Unsettled Homeland of Dreams, (All Things Matter Press),
winner of the Edna Ferber Fiction Award of 2019.

I am honored to learn the true story of Sgt. Peter Langlois. These personal letters from Vietnam to his family are immediate and real. Tears well up. I feel the deep fear, anger, and pain Peter felt. This book captures one soldier's willingness to serve, and the gripping heartache and loss experienced by an American family. I echo the words in his sister's poem, the words Peter didn't hear back then, "Welcome Home, Brother!"

— Jim Grunseth, 1974 West Point Graduate

For Judy,
In remembrance of our Vietnam Veterans

COMBAT *and* CAMPUS:

WRITING THROUGH WAR

by

SGT. PETER R. LANGLOIS

and

ANNETTE LANGLOIS GRUNSETH

Annette L. Grunseth

Published 2021
Printed in the United States of America
Photos by: Peter R. Langlois and Annette Langlois Grunseth

ISBN: 978-1-940863-12-2
Library of Congress Control Number: 2021934533

Cover and book design by Michelle Rich, Apothik Media & Design

ELM GROVE

FOREWORD

I am honored to add my own words and energy to the telling of a fellow Vietnam Veteran's "tour-of-duty" and his coming-of-age story. This brother-in-arms, "baby boomer", and a Purple Heart recipient, was also like me, a victim of PTSD and Agent Orange. This book is not just a story of Peter Langlois, but it is also the parallel history of that period through the eyes of his younger sister Annette. It captures, through his letters and those of the family, those turbulent times.

The deeper more spiritual emotions are best summarized through the softer lens by the poetry of his sister. She soulfully chronicles the moods, music and history of those who lived and walked through that painful time and place for our nation. Her experience is a collective experience for all those families who had relatives serving during that time.

The uncomfortable non-welcome home, that all of us got, from our country and even in our own communities, was soul killing. It was mentally worse than the war itself for us. We had expected our enemies to be shooting at us; but coming home to find that we were hated and treated as war criminals; that was what drove a hot knife through our hearts and souls. Rejection and a great lack of understanding along with the righteous judgment of the anti-war "heroes" was the breaking point for veterans. We were basically left alone to deal with our own wounds – both physically and emotionally. Our generation of veterans was abandoned and disregarded like yesterday's newspaper. Many of us never, ever, got over that!

All of us Vietnam veterans died there – some laid dead on the battle fields and the rest of us went home to die a little at a time from PTSD and the effects of Agent Orange. No one came back unchanged. No one was ever the same. Some of us could never truly leave that war behind us. We dealt with it in whatever ways we could. For some, that meant bouts with anger, nightmares, depression, booze, drugs, divorce, mental and physical health issues, and always spiritual and emotional pain. There were a few of us that grew, evolved, and learned to serve and give so we reached out to help support our own brothers. Unfortunately, there were too few giving and just too many in need. In the end, the only people Nam Vets could rely on for any assistance and understanding were themselves.

When Nam Vets get together, even if total strangers, we always say "Welcome Home Brother"! No one else did that for us, so we became our own welcoming committee. All of us understand and know who the veteran is; we do not need to know much more. He is our brother.

I read Peter and Annette's stories and I took that journey back with them through my memory of that part of my own life. I believe this book will do the same for other families and veterans. I think it will also create a better understanding for newer generations who were not there.

This collective of emotional snapshots may serve to help promote a more positive healing process for a nation who has still not fully dealt with the issues. That is truly my hope. It is never too late to be kind to each other. This nation has been divided too many times and for too long. It is now time for healing.

Sgt. Peter Langlois was a hero and he lived a life that should be honored. His story is just one of thousands. Before it is too late, I hope people reach out to them and hear their stories and listen to what they went through. It is not that far in the foreseeable future that these brave warriors will all be gone from the battle fields of life itself.

Welcome them all home!

— Rev. Bill McDonald
Founder of The Military Writers Society of America, Author, Award Winning Poet, Founder Spiritual Warrior's Ministry, Artist, International Inspirational & Motivational Speaker, Vietnam Veteran (Distinguished Flying Cross, Bronze Star, Purple Heart, 14 Air Medals)

ACKNOWLEDGEMENTS

This book could not have been possible without the sacrifice of my brother, Sgt. Peter R. Langlois, (July 19, 1945 – December 18, 2004) who served in Vietnam July 1968-69.

In loving remembrance of our parents Al and Betty Langlois, for their foresight to recognize the historical significance of Peter's letters, for preserving them, and encouraging me to publish this story.

I offer deep gratitude and love to my husband Sgt. John S. Grunseth, USAF, MACV, AFLS, Advisory Team 62, Saigon, Vietnam, 1969-1970, for his valuable knowledge of Vietnam, the military, and his support, including typing my brother's letters and scanning photos.

Special thanks and recognition to the immediate family of Peter Langlois for their love, stories, and inspiration.

Deep gratitude to author, Ruth W. Crocker, for our serendipitous meeting and for her suggestions and guidance. This book would not have been possible without her belief in its unique perspective and its importance in history.

Deep thanks to the Bjorklunden writers group led by Robin Chapman; and Beta readers, Thomas Davis, Andrew Grunseth, Anna Grunseth, James Grunseth, Anne Marie Langlois, Laura Langlois, Estella Lauter, and Tori Grant Welhouse.

A special thank you to copy editors Judy and Jim Kneiszel, The Word House, De Pere, Wisconsin, for their attention to detail, friendship, and support of this story.

Grateful appreciation to the following publications in which some of these poems appeared, in similar forms:

Bramble Lit Magazine, *Chopsticks, Pears*

Central Wisconsin HOOPLA, *The Inheritance*

Dispatches Magazine (Military Writers Society of America), *A Second Chance to Live, On Behalf of a Grateful Nation, Pears*

Fox Cry Review, *The Inheritance, Reflection*

The Mill, a Place for Writers, finalist, 2020 poetry contest, *On Behalf of a Grateful Nation*

No More Can Fit Into the Evening (Four Windows Press 2020) *Pears, My Mother's Moon*

Portage Magazine, *My Mother's Moon, Ongoing War, Invisible Wounds*

Poets to Come, Walt Whitman Bicentennial Anthology, *Olly, Olly, Oxen Free*

Wisconsin Fellowship of Poets Calendar, *Chopsticks*

First names mentioned in the letters written to neighbors and friends have been changed for privacy reasons.

Peter R. Langlois

INTRODUCTION

In 1967 my brother, Peter, who was five years older than I am, had just earned his bachelor's degree in journalism and advertising from the University of Wisconsin–Madison. Upon graduation Peter was classified 1-A with the draft. In addition, he had a low draft number and was immediately selected to receive his *greetings from your friends and neighbors and the President of the United States* draft letter.

What happened in the late 1960s shaped our lives. The things that happened to my brother forever changed him, my family, and me; each of us affected in our own way.

As a child, and in the following decades, I often thought about war: Why wars happen, how wars end, and how another war starts. I have wondered how people and governments of different countries and cultures can hate enough to kill each other and then, after a war has ended, the opposing countries become friendly, trade goods, and do business together.

When I was growing up, my mother told stories of her father serving in World War I as an Army captain and dentist in France. I heard her talk about World War II and how a ration book of stamps was required to purchase gasoline, sugar, and coffee. My mother enlisted in the Women's Auxiliary Army Corps in 1943 later known as the Women's Army Corps. My dad was a captain in the Army Air Forces. They met while both in the service and fell in love.

Mother related the story of how she could not purchase a white wedding dress for their 1944 wedding because all white fabric was allocated to making parachutes; she wore a lovely street dress instead. My mother's brother, on leave from the Army Air Forces, was the photographer on that special day. It would be the last time she ever saw him. In less than a year, he was declared missing in action over the Pacific.

Twenty-three years later, the loss of my mother's brother shadowed us as my parents' only son, and my only sibling, went off to yet another war, this one in Vietnam.

My brother, Peter, was born on July 19, 1945, thirteen months after D-Day, a turning point to ending WWII in Europe. He was given the middle name Richard, after my mother's brother, the uncle we would never know. I was born four and a half years later on December 3, 1949. We would grow up during the prosperous 1950s, a time when our country had stability and a feeling of upward mobility for the middle class.

Growing up in the 1950s

Walter Cronkite narrated The Twentieth Century, a television documentary series in the late 1950s. As a family we watched the programs which featured WWII films of planes dropping bombs, planes being shot down, and aircraft trying to land on carrier ships, often missing the mark, sliding into the ocean like the fighter planes from my brother's childhood games. I had trouble falling asleep as a child thinking about war and why people kill each other. I sometimes wondered if my uncle might walk through our door one day. Perhaps such an idea represented my own childish sort of hope.

At home, my parents talked about "The Red Scare", "The Cold War", and "The Iron Curtain" in the 1950s and early 1960s. As I ran my fingers over a globe that sat on my dad's desk, I innocently thought there was an actual iron curtain hanging between countries in Europe. Our middle-class life felt safe and comfortable and as a young child, I didn't fully grasp the threat that continued to be out there, on the other side of the world.

I vividly remember watching my older brother and his friends play "war games" on the dirt pile next door where a new house was being built. They dug trenches and created firing lines while making machine gun noises and jumping for cover in their foxholes. They created excitement shooting toy guns and throwing make-believe grenades at each other. We were learning about life, boys played "war" and we girls played "house." The 1960s and 1970s would drastically change those gendered stereotypes.

The 1960s: A Time of War and Anti-War.
As I entered high school in the mid-1960s, Vietnam dominated the news and conversations. I heard people say, if Vietnam falls to communism, communism will spread to Indonesia, Australia and eventually the United States. The news reported thousands of combat troops were landing in Vietnam. On the evening news we watched footage of U.S. soldiers and tanks rolling into combat against the Viet Cong.

As the Vietnam conflict intensified, draft numbers were drawn publicly on television, by birthdate, to select men for possible induction into military service. The military draft for Vietnam peaked in July 1965, as 35,000 young people were drafted in one month[1]. By the time my brother was drafted in 1967, our country was feeling war-weary as protests against the war were happening on campuses across the country. Some draftees were staging protests where they burned their draft cards. Bob Dylan captured it well with his popular song, *The Times They Are A-Changin'*.

When Peter drew a low draft number in June 1967 as he was graduating from college, he had planned to start his journalism career, but instead, like many young men his age, a number determined his fate.

Before reporting for basic training, Peter and his best friend had a final adventure. They took the family canoe, camping supplies, and headed to the wilderness of northern Canada. From June through late August, they paddled and portaged across most of Ontario, to Hudson Bay, then loaded their gear and the canoe on a freight train heading back to the United States. My parents and I wondered if he would stay in Canada, but Peter's sense of duty and pride as a citizen won out.

Turbulent Times

The anti-war movement was gaining momentum. In 1967 Martin Luther King, Jr. led a march in Chicago declaring his opposition to the war. In October thousands of anti-war protestors marched on the Pentagon in Washington, D.C. waving banners and chanting anti-war slogans. Meanwhile at our house on a quiet street in Wausau, Wisconsin, memories tugged at us about what had happened to my uncle in WWII as we watched television images of American soldiers fighting in the rice paddies of Vietnam. We agonized over what was going to happen to my brother, due to a draft number the United States government had given him.

Peter wrote 36 letters from 1967-69 from basic training to Officer Candidate School (OCS) and continuing through his year in Vietnam, July 1968 to July 1969, at the height of the war. He put his journalism skills to use and sent us first-person accounts with detailed descriptions of what he experienced along with his thoughts about the war.

As my brother prepared for combat with basic training and advanced infantry training, I was a busy high school senior with a class play, choir performances, senior prom, and bidding farewell to the only friends I knew, graduating on June 5, 1968. The world was changing fast. We were no longer children, and the peaceful prosperity of the 1950s was extinguished by unrest in our country. Our nation was divided into pro-war "hawks" and anti-war "doves."

Summer of 1968: A Hot Blur of Events

The summer of 1968 was a hot blur of unsettled turmoil and grief. My maternal grandmother passed away at age 73 on June 9 from a brain tumor, just four days after I graduated from high school. It was an election year compounded with war protests, divisiveness, and heatwaves. President Lyndon Johnson had earlier declared that he would not seek reelection for a second term.

Former U.S. Attorney General and New York Senator, Robert Kennedy, was a Democratic Party candidate for nomination for president. He was assassinated on June 5, 1968.

The Democratic National Convention in Chicago was targeted by thousands of anti-war protestors facing off with armed police. Riots for equal justice exploded in major cities in the months following Rev. Martin Luther King, Jr's April, 1968 assassination. Vietnam Veterans Against the War staged marches in Washington, D.C. where ex-soldiers led the way in wheelchairs.

As our family dealt with these tragedies of death, race riots, war protests, the upcoming election, and my preparing to leave for college, Peter was on his way to Vietnam, landing halfway around the world on July 18, 1968, the day before his 23rd birthday.

I was accepted to the University of Wisconsin–Madison, the

same university from which my brother had graduated. I left home in early September, 1968 to start my freshman year.

Flower Power, Make Love Not War

Going from a small town to the culturally expansive University of Wisconsin (UW) campus in Madison was exhilarating. I was meeting people from all over the world and taking interesting classes at a Big Ten school in the heart of a changing culture as protests on college campuses were peaking nationwide. Flower Power, Make Love Not War, and Hell No, We Won't Go were chanted at campus sit-ins and demonstrations protesting the war in Vietnam.

The UW campus protests included peace marches, teach-ins and sit-ins, but the intended peaceful demonstrations soon turned violent. During the fall semester of 1968, the National Guard was called in, dressed in riot gear, toting guns on their shoulders and wielding long white clubs. Violence erupted as students refused to disperse. Students and the National Guard clashed almost daily on University Avenue, a main thoroughfare, located outside my dormitory window.

From my fifth-floor window I saw students throwing rocks and bottles as the National Guard pushed back, swinging clubs, and sometimes wrestling students to the pavement. On my way to class, I followed a platoon of combat-ready National Guard, in full riot gear, marching up Bascom Hill, through the very heart of the campus. It was frightening to have military formations surrounding me while walking to class. I was determined to stay focused on my course work, achieve good grades, and not waste the money I had paid for tuition.

The War at Home

As the National Guard reached the top of the hill, they entered Bascom Hall, the iconic, main building on campus that also housed the office of the university chancellor. Guards holding rifles across their chests were positioned outside my Philosophy 101 classroom door. I felt intimidated, as they let me pass into my classroom where my professor and his dog "Henry" (the subject of philosophical discussions) greeted us with the day's lesson plan. I wondered how the National Guard could identify protestors from the peaceful students going to class. I concentrated on minding my own business, avoided skirmishes for my own safety, and for my mother, who was distressed with worry about Peter and about me.

National news coverage of Vietnam consisted of newspaper stories, news reported on radio stations, and, thanks to improving technologies, a growing number of television stations reporting war news as it was happening. Vietnam was the first "TV war," showing as-it-was-happening news coverage. News correspondents were on the ground alongside soldiers in Vietnam to film and report daily ambushes, bombings, gunfire, and casualties. Walter Cronkite, an anchor on the CBS television network, was a trusted, fatherly figure. We listened to his reports of air strikes by the North Vietnamese and the United States, both sides destroying cities, villages, and supply lines. Every day, Walter Cronkite sadly reported how many U.S. soldiers were killed in action.

Letters were the main form of communication. My brother, Sgt. Peter Langlois, used his journalism skills to report what he experienced in training and then in the jungles of Vietnam. He wrote graphic details in his letters where he foreshadowed what we have learned decades later — that this war was not winnable.

Making Peace with What Happened

My portion of this book includes two of my letters written to Peter and documentary poetry where I share and reflect on my time at UW–Madison, my brother's letters, and the years after he came home from Vietnam.

The Vietnam War has been over for more than a half century and is part of our nation's history. This is our family's story, but also the experience of many families like ours who persevered during the turbulent times of the 1960s. I am indebted to my parents Al and Betty Langlois who kept my brother's letters in a safe deposit box for decades. They recognized the historical importance of their son's eyewitness account of the war. As my mother was dying at age 91, in 2011, she expressed a final wish: "Please get Peter's letters published, his story needs to be told."

— Annette Langlois Grunseth (Sister of Sgt. Peter Langlois)

TABLE OF CONTENTS

In the letters you will encounter military jargon, acronyms, and soldier slang phrases specific to the Vietnam War. To maintain the integrity of the letters, the acronyms and phrases are explained in a glossary at the end of this book.

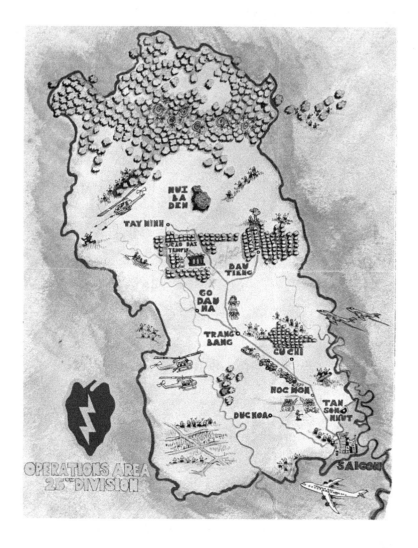

Operations area of Vietnam, Alpha Co. 2/22nd Infantry, 25th Division, Dau Tieng

Part One

BASIC TRAINING

Basic Training 1950s

My brother and his friends
dig a foxhole in the empty lot next door.

They dig deep, serious work,
piling heaps of brown dirt next to the hole.

They play war with wooden guns,
make gunfire noises with their mouths,

dive into the foxhole, guns flailing in the air,
olive green canteens fastened to their belts.

They see me on the sidewalk riding
a red and white tricycle,

pop out of the hole, run over to me.
My brother says he wants to show me something,

I go with him to the deep, square hole.
The boys coax me down inside with them.

Then they scramble, like green army men, up and out,
leaving me in the hole, a "prisoner of war."

Too little to climb the towering walls, I cry and scream
until mother runs out from the house

demanding my release, scolding my brother.
He's grounded. I am set free.

— Annette Langlois Grunseth

Olly, Olly Oxen Free

We played Robin Hood
in the trees across the street from our house
along the road to the old folks' home.
We trampled those dirt paths down to the lake
poked sticks in the water, hunted frogs,
exploring like Davy Crockett
our own wild frontier.

We spent hours along Lillie Street acting out
plays we made up in the
wooden gazebo on Zirbel's Point.
We climbed the rafters to watch bats sleeping,
brushed spiders out of our hair,
screaming through the cobwebs.

On hot July afternoons
we braided long silk scarves together,
pinned them to the back of our short summer hair,
like National Velvet, rode our bikes, (which we said were horses)
on paths we made in the field across the street
hot wind blowing through tall grass and our silky braids.

We rushed through dinner to run back outside for games,
"Red Light, Green Light...hope to see a ghost tonight"
Kick the Can, and S.P.U.D. As it grew dark,
my mother blew her whistle three times calling us home.
We chased each other in the twilight,
gasping to escape the ghost as street lights flickered.
Olly, Olly Oxen Free!

— Annette Langlois Grunseth

FORT DIX
New Jersey

BASIC TRAINING &

ADVANCED INFANTRY TRAINING

FORT DIX NEW JERSEY

"It's a real test of character." — Peter Langlois

November – December 1967

10 November 1967

Dear Mom, Dad, and Annette,

So much has happened since the last time I talked to you that I hardly know where to start. First of all, I graduated from basic training last Wednesday so I'm past the first stage in my training. Looking back on the past eight weeks I've decided that basic was much easier than I expected.

I moved to my AIT unit yesterday in high spirits expecting a weekend pass and a lot less harassment than basic, but had a rude awakening. First of all, the quarters are very old and in poor repair. And to make matters worse, the NCO's are making our first few days in basic seem like a push over. Upon arriving at the new unit, we were informed that there would be no weekend passes and no post privileges. This in itself was a major disappointment when it's normally the custom to have a 3-day pass at the end of basic. However, we did get post privileges today but we had to earn these the hard way (the entire barracks had to be scrubbed first, boots shined, and lockers squared away) before anyone could leave the company area.

There's a chin-up bar outside the mess hall entrance and the only way you can eat is to do the number of chin-ups asked for first. In a tight resume my first impression of AIT is not too positive. It just seems to be another nightmare starting over again – only worse.

During basic training, squad and platoon spirit got everyone through the tough times. So at the moment everyone in my new platoon is trying to reassure the fellow sleeping next to him that AIT really isn't all that bad. At any rate I'm sure it's only a matter of time before the NCOs start smiling and acting human.

Each platoon lives in one large room (about 50 people) that is separated into "bays" with four bunks in each bay. Two of the fellows in my bay were in my old company so at least we are starting

16

with people we know. I'll keep you posted on the training after it gets underway this coming Monday.

AIT is designed as a prep school for OCS so naturally the discipline is tighter and more is expected of everyone because the majority of us are college grads and signed up for OCS. That accounts for the hell there was to pay the first day here.

Each OCS applicant gets a chance to run a squad, platoon, and the company in field exercises during the next 8 weeks. I just hope I don't blow my first lesson in leadership when my turn comes up. The one thing that really has become evident about the Army so far is that it's a real test of character. You have to keep telling yourself you're good enough to make it – all the way to the end of OCS. The last two months were not all that easy but the next 2 months look much tougher. I can imagine what OCS holds in store.

If you haven't already, please have my skis repaired as soon as possible. Although I'm not sure, I think my Christmas leave starts Dec. 16th. I'll try to find out definitely so you can perhaps arrange for plane tickets.

Much love,

Peter

Sunday – 26 November 1967

Dear Mom, Dad and Annette

Thank you for arranging for Christmas airline reservations. It is really a load off my mind to have things settled.

You are probably wondering why in my previous letters nothing was mentioned about the news clipping and the pictures of the boat. That particular letter was post marked November 7th but I did not receive it until the middle of the past week. On Nov. 9th I moved to AIT so the letter which was addressed to my BCT unit, had to be forwarded. However, it was forwarded to the wrong AIT Company, then to the Post postal locator, and then finally to me. I guess this is nothing unusual though for the Army just another case of SOP at its slowest. At any rate I'm grateful for the pictures and the fishing news. When are you going to paint the name on the boat? I noticed in the pictures that the stern was still bare.

This week Delta Company was on bivouac and to put it bluntly it was cold as hell. The one consolation is that we don't have to use pup tents. The bivouac area is set up with large wall tents that have 2 stoves, regular bunk beds and a cement floor. I might add that the cold cement floor really wakes you up fast when you jump out of bed at 4 a.m.

After breakfast each day we marched to the machine gun range and spent the whole week learning to shoot it and take it apart. Everyone enjoyed firing and got big thrills out of shooting just about everything in sight. One fellow had a malfunction – his machine wouldn't stop until the ammo was gone – he held on while a 200 round belt went through the gun.

This week we'll be on bivouac again qualifying with the fully automatic version of the M-14. The way the schedule has been set up, the only time you bathe is in the barracks during the weekend. To say the least, it smelled like there was something rotten in Denmark when we came in from the field.

I hope you all had a pleasant Thanksgiving. Our Company commander let us come in from bivouac for the day to have a turkey dinner. And it tasted great. Of course, anything beats the "slop" we get during bivouac.

I will make it a point to contact the fellow whose name you sent. Since he is in basic, I'll be able to compare impressions with him on the way home.

By the way, I intend to follow through with OCS. Now that I've grown more accustomed to the Army, I don't see why I can't make it. Also, from what I've seen, the Army would be nothing more than a dead three years for me unless I made it through OCS and became an officer. In other words, I simply feel my time is valuable enough to be doing something constructive with it and OCS seems to be a means to this end.

As you can probably guess, I'm anxious to get home and literally I am counting the days until Dec. 15th. The best part of the leave will be watching Fort Dix disappear behind the bus to Philadelphia. Will you also dry clean my ski pants and jacket? And thanks for taking my skis in for repairs.

I had a pass this weekend so I went into Trenton with a couple guys from my platoon. The town was amazingly cordial to servicemen and we all had a great time.

Much love,

Peter

Christmas 1967, Wausau, WI, Peter Langlois on leave after Basic Training

Sunday 7 January 1968

Dear Mom, Dad, and Annette,

After a lot of fooling around with the airlines, I made it back to good ol' Fort Dix last Tuesday with only minutes to spare. The leave ended at 5 p.m. and I signed in at 4:52 p.m. I must admit I was pretty nervous all that afternoon.

My North Central flight from Wausau got into Milwaukee just as my Northwest connection to Philadelphia was taking off. Consequently, North Central put me on standby out of Chicago on TWA. When I got to O'Hare TWA was announcing a flight departing for Philly so I went to the TWA gate and bingo, I got the last available seat. If I had waited for a seat on the TWA flight North Central had arranged for me, I would have been several hours late. As it turned out, I was put on a detail in the mess hall as soon as I reported in. Some welcome, some Happy New Year and one hell of a way to end a leave.

Yesterday we had a big company I.G. inspection; in fact, we never went to bed at all Friday night preparing for it. For that matter we were up until mid-night Tuesday, Wednesday, and Thursday polishing and cleaning and then getting up at 4 a.m. to march out to the 50-cal. machine gun range.

Naturally, everyone was looking forward to weekend passes but the CO restricted a good 2/3 of the company for not getting short haircuts. Luckily, I did, so I had a pass.

I went with 3 other guys from the company to Lakewood, New Jersey, about 50 miles east of Fort Dix. All we did was look for a destination on the road map and quickly got away from Fort Dix. We checked into a motel about 2:30 p.m., bought a bottle, and watched football games all afternoon. About 6 p.m. we decided to go out on the town as soon as the Jackie Gleason Show was over. However, the week had taken its toll. I fell asleep as did the rest and never woke up until 7:00 a.m. this morning. All of us, of course never ate anything last night so we ate a huge breakfast and came back to Fort Dix at 2 p.m. This might not sound very exciting but we discovered a nice inexpensive, quiet town and had the chance to catch up on much needed sleep.

Still no word on OCS starting date. I'll keep you posted. Thanks again for a very enjoyable Christmas. I do not think I have ever appreciated being home more than I did the last several weeks.

Much love,

Peter

OFFICER CANDIDATE SCHOOL
Fort Benning, Georgia

JANUARY - MAY 1968

"We were informed that most of us would be going to Vietnam as platoon leaders in the infantry."
– Peter Langlois

Sunday 28 January 1968

Dear Mom, Dad, & Annette,

Greetings from the Benning School for Boys. OCS is everything I expected and a heck of a lot more that I did not expect. Pressure, tension, stress, and harassment are with you all the time. I'm thoroughly amazed at what is expected of you in very limited periods of time.

Frankly, the most prevalent problem in the 96th Company is constipation due to the extreme tension and pressure. I dare say you cannot walk from your room down the hall to the latrine without someone bracing you up against the wall for some sort of chewing out. But, as bad as this may sound, I must admit the ranting and raving doesn't bother me.

What I really dislike is the demanding rigidity – everything spit shined and polished in a certain place in your room. It's a 24 hour a day job to keep the room straight. The SOP for the room is very detailed and as hard as I try, the platoon tactical officer blows his mind every time he inspects the room – of course he does with everyone else too so I don't feel too bad about it.

The other big bugaboo is the mess hall. We have to eat meals at attention, sitting on the first three inches of the chair. While eating, the tactical officers and the senior OCS candidates harass you, ask silly questions requiring just as silly memorized answers, and dish out push-ups, sit-ups, and knee bends for anyone caught eye balling. In short, it's just one big horror.

One thing I must admit is that, although standards are high, there are no impossible or unjust things required of you. The big problem primarily is organizing your time and that's right down to the last minute.

Secondly, in comparison to Fort Dix, Fort Benning is very modern and beautifully landscaped. The classrooms and the instructors are just as adequate and capable as anything I associated with at the University of Wisconsin.

I have to praise the OCS set-up because it is so well run and organized that I'm sure it will be the most informative and maturing experience I've ever had. The reason I'm saying this is that I've never been confronted with a more difficult task. It takes guts just to get out of bed in the morning knowing what's ahead of you for the day.

OCs are required to buy a number of extra items the first week of training such as uniforms, jump boots, etc. Consequently, I found myself short on money so I arranged for a $50 loan from the Columbus Bank and Trust Company. I've also set-up a checking account with them and arranged for my monthly salary check to be sent there for deposit to my account.

I'm confident this will be a very workable arrangement.

The 18th week of training the 96th Co. will be in senior status. At this point you're granted all the privileges of an officer. Until then, we're very restricted as to where we can go and what we can do. For instance, I never heard anything about the Korean situation[2] until yesterday. Therefore, could you send me a book of stamps so I can keep on writing? I have no more [stamps] left and have no idea when or where I'll have a chance to get out of here for some.

One thing I'm rather distressed about is that the other day we were informed that most of us would be going to Vietnam as platoon leaders in the infantry. Branch transfers to Adjutant Generals Corp, etc. which I had hoped for have been banned. However, you can still apply and pray for luck in getting into military intelligence. This I'm doing but the prospects are not very good that I'll be able to get accepted. The infantry, combat, and Vietnam just don't seem to hold much security for the future. I hate to stop here on such a dismal note but I have to prepare my equipment for drill and ceremonies class this afternoon. Please write often, it's the only contact any of us have with the outside world.

Much love,

Peter

4 February 1968

Dear Mom, Dad, and Annette,

First of all, Happy Birthday Dad. I'm sorry I couldn't send you a gift or card but you just cannot get out of the 96th company area as a new OC. We're so busy that everyone forgets the time and day of the week. It's just a matter of living from day to day and hour to hour.

There is a tremendous psychological element to OCS. The "tact" officers tell us one thing and one day after, the SOP is entirely different. There's no remedy other than to stay loose and take it as it comes. The day starts at 5:30 a.m. and lights are out at 10:30 p.m. But I'm not exaggerating when I say that you're damn lucky if you can work in a quick shower. There are millions of details to be taken care of constantly and frankly it's driving me batty.

Junior OCs never walk or march. Double time is SOP. We run every morning (about 1 mile) to the PT field where the Ranger Training Command takes over and sweats us to a frazzle.

The airborne training area is directly across the street from our barracks. Each afternoon before supper we run from 1-3 laps on the airborne track which is 1 1/4 miles long, both up and down hill. I'd venture to say I've lost 7 or 8 pounds already. Please write and use the right address next time.

Much love,

Peter

18 March 1968

Dear Mom, Dad, and Annette,

As you can probably tell from the frequency of my letters, I've been extremely busy. I received your letters early last week while on bivouac and had to read them by firelight while on guard duty at 0300 in the morning.

I'm glad to hear that Annette has not resigned herself to "old maid" status. Tell her to look in the mirror if she needs anymore confidence about her feminine appeal. Is this boy the intellectual type, a muscular "jock," or just a groovy guy with greasy kid's stuff on his hair? All fun aside, I'm happy to find out that boys are replacing all those idiot solitaire games.

Our bivouac last week ended up as great fun but the beginning was pure hell. We marched to the bivouac area with full field gear – pistol belt, canteen, pack, sleeping bag, tent, ammo pouches, shovel, bayonet, steel helmet, and rifle. In the process of getting there we were attacked several times by "aggressor forces" and then had to counter attack. What it amounted to was one hell of a lot of double timing. With all the weight we were carrying it was a real ordeal.

The bivouac area was in Alabama, about ten miles west of the Chattahoochee River, the state line and western border of Fort Benning. While in the field, I slept with long underwear on because there was frost every night. Even now, we're still wearing jackets, but sources say the famous Georgia heat will start in a month or so.

Big deal, yesterday his royal majesty, the company commander, gave us smoking privileges. However, the discipline remains super strict. We cannot walk on the floors in our rooms because they have to be spit shined at all times as do boots, shoes, and belt buckles – including the front, back, and inside of the buckle. It seems like everything is for "display purposes only." The urinals in the latrine are never used because they must be ready for inspection at all times – even when we're getting dressed in the morning. Waste baskets can't be used because they also must be highly polished. Someone's always watching and when you least expect it, a "tact" officer pops up and starts ranting about how "gross" or "sorry" you or your equipment looks. The Benning School for Boys has all the characteristics of the local zoo at feeding time. Utter chaos will prevail, then everyone gets organized and boom the SOP changes and you start all over.

As a reaction, everyone in the platoon has grouped tightly together as well as the entire company to fight the menace. As a revolt, we had beer and hot dogs delivered to our bivouac the last night in the field. It was the 1st time we have put one over on the cadre and they thought it was great. The goodies were a real treat because normally all hell breaks out if you're caught eating anything outside the mess hall. Needless to say there have been many ingenious methods devised to smuggle in food.

By the way, I applied for military intelligence. The application went in last week. I'm hoping like heck it goes through because it appears to be the only way out of the infantry.

Write Soon – Send Food (that's legal)

Much love,

Peter

P.S. Graduation date is 5 July – 5 weeks done, 18 left (groan)

"Much to my own disappointment...."
– Peter Langlois

20 April 68

Dear Mom, Dad, and Annette,

I hope "you all" had a good time while you were "way down yonder in Dixie." I have grown to be quite fond of Georgia in the past thirteen weeks, probably because the environment in the Columbus area is so similar to Wisconsin. That is, the countryside is similar not the infernal heat. It was 90 degrees here today and I long for the cool northern evenings.

I wish I could speak as cheerfully about OCS. Previously I was very enthusiastic but I guess that was while OCS was still a very extreme but novel experience. Since I last wrote, the program has settled into a terrible routine, everything planned according to SOP from 0530 to 2230 every day. In short, the OCS program has become for me a very dull and unexciting bore.

Consequently, my attitude has traveled the continuum from positivism to complete negativism. I realize the following remarks will disappoint you and others who have been pulling for me to receive a commission but my most recent actions I did for myself, and me only, because I feel I know my potential and capabilities better than anyone else. By now you may have already guessed what I'm about to say. That is, much to my own disappointment, I resigned from the OCS program today.

There have been many circumstances leading to this decision and I feel I owe you some explanation. First of all, the physical harassment which I groaned over previously tapered off to nothing and presented no problem. However, mentally, my mind has been run through a meat grinder. In the beginning everyone makes mistakes, however, my progress at correcting these mistakes has been slow and difficult. In short, I find I was from the start not mentally prepared for the emotional stress that is the backbone of OCS.

Secondly, I have been informed that I would be commissioned in the infantry. At the same time my tactical officer and the company commander have said I do not display the characteristics they are looking for in a combat leader.

Thirdly, I am tired and bored with being set up as an example of what not to be in front of my platoon and the company. The final blow came today. Today, 96th Company reached the intermediate phase of OCS. It is celebrated with one hell of a big party full of high-ranking officers etc. The party also serves as a training vehicle for familiarization with social conduct i.e. receiving lines, sit down dinner, the whole bit. A date committee was organized about 4 weeks ago to get blind dates from nearby colleges since no one has a chance to get off post and socialize with the Columbus belles.

Previously, we had an informal party in our eighth week in which dates were arranged the same way. At that time, I had a date with a blasé character from Wesleyan College in Atlanta. However, the Wesleyan girls finked out for this party today because of exams following Easter vacation. Consequently, the date committee went to Auburn College and the streets of Columbus for dates. I was set up with a girl from Converse College in South Carolina as were 3 other candidates who had dates arranged from the same school.

At 11 o'clock this morning, my date called and said she could not come. At noon, during a company formation, the executive officer, inquired who did not have a date of those people not married or engaged. I was the only one in the company and the tactical officer took this as a cue for fun and games. I was "labeled" an "ugly social dud" in front of 160 people and given the direct order, "you will have something female at the party tonight." I spent the afternoon scrounging around motel swimming pools and Columbus bars to no avail. At the last place I went to I ran into my tactical officer and told him the situation. He replied, "You just blew the biggest social event of OCS. Obviously, you don't want to remain in the program."

My explanation did not suit him and after a discussion of my progress in the program I told him that my values and personality were the only thing the Army has not painted OD. And that I was not willing to display the animal like qualities that we've been taught that are synonymous with being a platoon combat leader. This was not a hasty decision, because thoughts along this line have occupied my mind for several weeks. The ridicule today finally broke me. Say it – your son cracked – I don't give a damn and I know that in 13 months I'll be a civilian and that really is all that matters to me now.

Peter

[Letter to Peter from his Dad]

Wed. April 24, 1968

Dear Pete:

Wow...your letter sure was a surprise. I thought you were getting along great and doing well in the program. I am not disappointed and I don't blame you in any way for your resignation. I think you have to handle these matters yourself. My only interest in the OCS program was in tying you up for 6 months so you wouldn't be exposed to anything more dangerous....and of course, it meant you might have some advantages as an officer that you would not have as an enlisted man.

One should never have any illusions about the army. They are not training you to pick daisies. They are training you to be an animal as you stated, but this is what war is about, a conflict between animals. The story you tell about the party and what they did when you [didn't get] your date is ridiculous, but of course, you got the reaction of one man and I wouldn't say his handling of the matter was very intelligent. He handled it in the army way and by now you should not be surprised by anything.

The big question you left unanswered, however, is what happens to you now. Surely you must have some idea. You will be reassigned and what will it be. Do you have any choices or do they stick a gun in your hand and put you in the front line. Please answer this question immediately.

Explore the possibility of going to school somewhere. There must be some training programs for which you can apply. What would happen if you checked all the possible fields and then applied for school? Look into this and let me know.

Annette is in the school play and I have promised to go, so I must run. I'll try to get a note off to you tomorrow and with some news about Mimi and mother, and the boat, etc.

Best Love,

Dad

32

Sunday, 5 May 1968

Dear Mom, Dad, & Annette,

It has been two weeks since I resigned from OCS, but I am still at 96th company. These two weeks have really been frustrating because I'm still required to perform and train as everyone else. Until I receive new orders for reassignment, I'll be here "playing" OCS. Depression isn't the word to describe my frame of mind but it probably gives some indication of the situation.

Most likely I will go from 96th company to 1st casual company next door. This is a holding company where OCS rejects and drop-outs, airborne dropouts, and personnel on physical profiles are sent to await further orders for a new duty station. This has been the procedure for the 63 people who have already left 96th company. It usually takes another 4-5 weeks to get new orders and most of these have been for Vietnam. SOP calls for a 30 day leave before going overseas in most cases. That's what's happening to former members of 96th company. However, I have been told nothing and know absolutely nothing about when I'll leave 96th and where I'll go from there. I can't recall ever being in a more depressing and insecure situation. Frankly, I'm fed up completely with the whole damn Army but I imagine this attitude will change when I get the heck out of OCS.

The news about Mimi came as a complete surprise. I had no idea that she was so seriously ill. Naturally, I'm in a rather ambiguous situation here but if she should pass away as you say she might, maybe I can get some sort of leave to come home. That's one leave I hope is never necessary.

Much love,

Peter

[Mimi is Peter's maternal grandmother]

CASUAL COMPANY
Fort Benning, Georgia

WAITING AND MORE WAITING

MAY – JUNE 1968

*"No one here has anything to look
forward to except Vietnam."*
– Peter Langlois

10 May 1968
Fort Benning, Georgia

Dear Mom, Dad, and Annette,

I am finally out of OCS. As I expected, I was moved to 1st Casual Company to await further orders. It's really an understatement to call this place the Army. Just the opposite extreme from OCS. There is much idle, boring time and no discipline whatsoever.

This morning I saw a dentist for a long overdue check-up. I'll be able to get the necessary work done with all my spare time.

I have attempted to get into something besides infantry but the policy is that OCS dropouts must reenlist if they want to change their MOS. Otherwise, it takes real political pull. Therefore, my MOS remains 11B10 i.e., infantry rifleman.

As yet, I have not been put on alert for overseas but that probably will come within the week. This is SOP with just about everyone. Unfortunately, the great majority are being shipped to the replacement center at Long Binh, Vietnam or Cam Ranh Bay. I requested a 30-day leave and put Alaska down for 1st preference for reassignment but it's doubtful I will get this.

As for Georgia and the Army – hot – dull – meaningless. Apathy prevails throughout the company and little if anything constructive gets accomplished. The whole bit drags on and on. Hopefully I'll be home sometime in June which would be a blessing. Any news on Mimi?

Much love,

Peter

20 May 1968

Fort Benning, Georgia

Dear Mom, Dad, and Annette,

I received an alert for Vietnam last Friday. This is the news I've been expecting and dreaded. At any rate there's no more suspense about my future disposition in the Army.

Before I can leave Fort Benning, I have to complete a week of overseas orientation. This training was supposed to start today but about 20 people including myself were rescheduled for orientation next week because the class was too big. If my orders for a leave come through next week, it will mean that I'll have to spend my first week of leave at Ft. Benning. This isn't likely but it has happened.

My alert states the address, "Vietnam Transient Detachment" APO San Francisco 96384. That zip code is for Long Binh, Vietnam which is a replacement center. So much for the bad news.

This past weekend I had a 3-day pass which I used to go to Atlanta. As I found out, Atlanta is a beautiful modern city and I enjoyed it thoroughly. Saturday night I saw a tremendous movie, "Gone With The Wind." Ironically the previous afternoon I went to a place called "cyclorama" where the battle of Atlanta is reenacted. These two experiences combined into a very informative history lesson.

Saturday evening, I also had another funny adventure. I ate dinner at a Polynesian restaurant where the only silverware used is chopsticks. After the initial fumbling and frustration, I became proficient with everything but eating rice with chopsticks and ended up using a spoon, much to the amusement of the waitress.

So, I'm still sitting, sleeping and generally doing nothing constructive except getting a suntan in Casual Company. This seems like the most useless waste of time I've ever spent anywhere. I just hope that my overseas orientation doesn't delay my processing any longer than is usually necessary.

Hopefully I'll be home within 3 or 4 weeks for a leave, however, I still must wait and wait for the damn red tape process to produce something for me.

Best love,

Peter

PS Send some "Civies" if you already have not

4 June 1968
Fort Benning, Georgia

Dear Mom, Dad, and Annette,

I don't know what the weather is like at home, but I'm sure you wouldn't want to be in Georgia. The temperature has been in the low 90's every day for two weeks with humidity to match. To make matters worse, the fans don't work in our old run-down barracks so it's extremely damp and stuffy constantly. A continuous night's sleep is not physically possible.

Recently, I have been reading up on Vietnam, primarily because the Post library is air conditioned. Peak temperatures in Vietnam are in the months of July and August – just about the time I'll be getting there. Lucky me. So far, I find Georgia unbearable. The thought of Vietnam and 100+ temperatures really scares me – I think even more than the idea of being under fire.

A new list of leave dates was posted today, however, my name wasn't on it. Later this week another list will be out and with luck

I'll be home around the latter part of June. At the same time, I can't help but wonder if the Army knows I exist. I cannot describe in words how uncomfortable, frustrating, and boring Causal Company really is. It's just a living hell filled with some of the greatest guys I've ever met and at the same time with the most degenerate trash I've ever seen. No distinction is made by the cadre, however, so everyone is more or less like an animal in the zoo – fed three meals a day and kept warm and breathing and that's all.

What's bad about Causal Company is that no one here has anything to look forward to except Vietnam. As a result, the people here display gross apathy toward each other and the Army.

I found how exciting being alive could be when I was at the UW because I had found myself and had goals to work for. The only goal I have now is to stay alive in the next year so as to protect what I have worked for. I'll fight like hell, but for my own personal survival, not for the cause I don't believe in or for the glory of military victory. This means nothing to me but my thoughts on the matter remain staunch. Army doctrine is the cheapest form of propaganda around, and frankly my week of Vietnam orientation was the biggest farce I have ever been involved in. It's no damn wonder the war has progressed so slowly.

How about a word from your end one of these weeks?

Much love,

Peter

Part Two

"…everything smells like garbage,
including your body because of the heat and humidity."
– Peter Langlois

Poems in Response
By
Annette Langlois Grunseth

[Arrival in Vietnam, 18 July was the day before Peter's 23rd birthday, 19 July. Written on a greeting card, 25th Infantry Division, Tropic Lightning]

July 1968

Dear Mom, Dad, Annette,

I had a great time in San Francisco & really hated to leave it. Sunday, I took a Grayline city tour and spent the rest of the day at Fisherman's Wharf – then rode a cable car back to the hotel.

The flight to Vietnam took 22 hours – arrived 1 p.m. 18 July. We flew from Travis AFB to Honolulu, to Clark AFB Manila, to Bien Hoa AFB – 22 miles northeast of Saigon. Now I'm at Cu Chi (20 miles NW of Saigon) waiting to be shipped to my new company.

Vietnam is terrible – everything smells like garbage, including your body because of the heat and humidity.

Best love,

Peter

TET OFFENSIVE 1968

It is important to know the history of when Peter landed in Vietnam, July, 1968. One of the biggest offensive attacks by the Communist North Vietnamese was in January 1968 at the Lunar New Year, called Tet, a major holiday in Vietnam. An extensive enemy military effort was coordinated, attacking numerous key targets simultaneously in South Vietnam. The North Vietnamese had hoped this concentrated effort would result in a victory to end the war. Attacks were directed in areas of heavy population in the south and a high concentration of U.S. Troops.

Wide-spread attacks by the North Vietnamese continued in a second phase during May, 1968, and a third phase of intense attacks occurred in South Vietnam during June, July, and August, 1968. Peter arrived in Vietnam in the middle of this heated warfare. There were massive losses of soldiers on both sides. The combat situations and ambushes that Peter experienced were at the peak of these attacks as a result of Tet Offensive. It was terrifying for everyone.

In the aftermath of this bloodshed in Vietnam, citizens of our country were losing faith in the United States' ability to win this war. Protests erupted across the country, especially on college campuses. President Lyndon B. Johnson and military advisers sent more troops thinking we could keep fighting and win this war. It became a very controversial issue in the United States with our leadership wanting to keep up the fight and many of the American people opposing the escalation of war. In March of 1968, President Johnson decided to not run for a second term as President. The election of November 1968 went to Richard Nixon who inherited the very difficult Vietnam War.

Source: Office of the Historian, Foreign Service Institute. United States Department of State.

The Arrival

Vietnam – my brother's first letter
Stinking
Steamy
No privacy
No doors
No locks
No Barracks
Bunkers
Few possessions
Nothing to gain
Everything to lose

Madison – me on campus
Freshman
Cool autumn air
Red and yellow trees
Marching band
Football
New faces every day
Dorm room
My own door with a lock
Good roommate
Textbooks
Notebooks
Everything to gain
Nothing to lose

— Annette Langlois Grunseth

(Mail from U.S. to Vietnam takes four days)

Saturday 3 August 1968

Dear Mom, Dad, and Annette,

Thanks much for writing. Mail is one of the few contacts G.I.s in Vietnam have with the "world."

I spent 5 days at Cu Chi taking a refresher course on how to stay alive in Vietnam. From there I was flown to Dau Tieng near the Cambodian border. This is the rear base camp for the 2/22 infantry. I only stayed there overnight, long enough to be issued my M-16 and field gear.

The next day I flew over to Ton Son Nhut Air Base in Saigon. My entire battalion is set up in a perimeter defense around the airport and the outskirts of Saigon since they're expecting another NVA offensive here any time.

The 2/22 Infantry is mechanized. In other words, the primary means of movement is with armored personnel carriers ("tracks"). There is one APC for each squad within a platoon so in one company, there are 16 APCs, each with a 50-cal. machine gun and 2 M60's. Everyone but the driver rides on top of the APC because the inside area gets completely blown to hell if the track hits a mine in the road. The APC also serves as the squad's house. We sleep eight men in our track at extreme close quarters. Hammocks, and ammo cans seem to make the best beds.

Normally, my company operates up north near Trang Bang but the monsoon season is in progress now and it's too muddy for major offensive operations with the tracks. So for now and probably until the end of November, we'll be camped in the mud (knee deep in spots) outside the air base. My company is also the reaction force for the U.S. Embassy in Saigon. If the NVA hit the city again we will be air lifted into the embassy to provide security.

During the day we clean weapons and take it easy. However, every night we go out on ambush patrols and set-up waiting to nail any VC or NVA trying to probe the perimeter. I will admit it scares the hell out of me. There's a 7:00 p.m. curfew in this area so anyone we see coming through our ambush site gets zapped. So far we haven't made any direct contact although occasionally the enemy mortars our "logger site" where the tracks stay during the day.

[Mail from U.S. to
VN takes four days] Sat. 3 Aug 68

Dear Mom, Dad, and Annette,
Thanks much for writing. Mail is one of the few contacts G.I.'s in Viet Nam have with the "world." I spent 5 days at Cu Chi taking a refresher course on how to stay alive in Viet Nam. From there I was flown to Dau Tieng near the Cambodian border. This is the rear base camp for the 2/22 infantry. I only stayed there overnight, long enough to be issued my M-16 and field gear. The next day I flew over to Ton Son Nhut (spelling?) Air base in Saigon. My entire battalion is set up in a perimeter defense around the airport and the outskirts of Saigon since they're expecting another NVA offensive here any time. The 2/22 infantry is mechanized. In other

Sometimes, we have a daytime mission. Three days ago we rode the tracks about 10 miles out into the rice paddies, then dis-mounted and waded into the paddies about 3000 meters in order to provide a blocking force for another unit's operation. We were about ¼ mile behind the battle area but could see everything that was happening. I'm still shaking from the experience. The unit in contact with the VC was going to drive the enemy into our position for an ambush if things got out of hand. Thank God it never happened. We could hear the mortars and artillery shells whistling over us; complete with rockets and machine guns, and jets with napalm made for quite a display. At any rate, the VC were wiped out and we never had to react to the other units for support.

Last night I was on an ambush patrol in the rain. More than likely each night is spent sitting out in the boondocks and getting soaked. We can't use ponchos because they reflect light and are noisy – this might give away our position, so we just wear jungle fatigues and no underwear – helps dry you out faster. At any rate, last night it was pouring like hell so the patrol leader decided to set up the ambush in a Vietnamese "Hootch" i.e. thatched house the locals call home. The people who lived there set up sleeping platforms for most of us and were very helpful and friendly. I spent the night behind a machine gun set up in the front doorway.

Our "logger site" is in a rice paddy so you can imagine how muddy it is. The gook children are around all day trading cold soda and ice for "chop chop" i.e. C rations. A few enterprising girls have set up a "boom boom" house outside the perimeter; however, the CO threatens an instant court martial for anyone he catches there.

So that's what Vietnam has been like so far - hot, smelly, muddy, wet, rainy. Whoever said "war is hell" was absolutely right. I'm sure when God created earth he forgot about Vietnam. It is just a stink hole of a place full of vermin and filth. I swear I'll kiss the ground when I get back to U.S. soil.

Of course, everyone here seems to be good sports and everyone

Left: C rations - prepared and canned food used when fresh food was not readily available.

Below: Tamed monkey, "Tiger" boosts morale in the 2/22nd Infantry

acts and treats his fellow soldier like a brother. We find humor one way or another with everything to keep our minds off the tragedy and the idiocy of this war. One of the fellows in my squad bought a baby monkey from the gooks and tamed it for several months. I swear the little "imp" is human. He sits up in the top of the 50-caliber turret when we're moving with the tracks. On smooth portions of the road he'll sometimes perch right on the barrel. As

I'm writing, Tiger is perched on my shoulder picking my ears and scratching my head for me. I hope when I get a camera I can send you some pictures of him and the rest of this madness.

Things I need:

1. Rubberized rain suit (parka and pants) with zipper or snaps on front of the parka. (Most of the guys have sent home for this item.)

2. Plastic case to put writing material in (zipper type plastic envelope).

Much love,

Peter

In the Shadow of Death 1968

Lo, though I walk through the valley
of the shadow of death
I shall fear no evil
for I am the evilest
son of a bitch in the Valley
is inscribed on a Zippo lighter
my brother bought at the PX
on his way to the jungle near Dau Tieng.
Many G.I.s carried one,
rubbed shiny in their pockets:
Talisman for soldiers,
some still in their teens.

— Annette Langlois Grunseth

16 August 1968
Late P.M.

Dear Mom, Dad, and Annette,

I really enjoyed hearing the news about the sailboat. It sort of tears me up though because I can't be home enjoying it with you.

Things are very much the same here since I last wrote – in fact, it's getting very routine. I think I'm pretty much acclimated except for one thing – sunburn.

The sun is so intense that I just keep burning and peeling every day. As a result, the guys in my platoon have nicknamed me "Red." My lower leg has been blistered and infected for several weeks and the medic finally sent me in to the 3rd Army Field Hospital in Saigon to see a doctor. The "Doc" gave me an ointment that has just about cleared up the problem.

However, the trip to the hospital was quite unnerving. While I was there, 6 medevac helicopters came in from the Delta with casualties. Each was covered with mud, bandages, and blood. Seeing this sort of thing in a magazine picture is totally different than being there to see it in person. I hope like hell I never make a trip to Saigon that way.

As for glasses, it takes several months to get them here. I have my own sunglasses in addition to the Army pair. I could send the Army sunglasses and have you get clear lenses for them. This is the only way to get any frames without sending back to the states – that takes forever thru Army Channels.

Earlier this week, Alpha and Bravo Companies of the 2/22 Inf. made a sweep near Cu Chi. Our sister company Bravo, made light contact and captured one VC. He looked about 20 but turned out to be 40 years old.

We're still going out on ambush patrols every night – still no contact at night. Last night my company surrounded a nearby village while the ARVNs made a "snatch" i.e. door to door VC hunt. They came out with five suspects and a few draft-aged men. The Vietnamese draft system works only at night and by surprise. Think what our hippies would make of that.

As I've explained, this is the monsoon season. Two nights ago, we had four tracks stuck in the mud in our "logger site." It took six tracks hooked together to pull each one out. The rice paddies keep getting deeper and harder to handle. Chest deep water is not unusual during our daylight sweep operations.

Now for more encouraging news. The battalion information specialist leaves RVN in November. After talking to him recently, he said I'd stand a good chance of being his replacement.

If that should happen, I'll probably be off the line by the end of October. But you know the Army – my journalism school degree probably means nothing. I'll believe it when I get the job – if that should happen.

Were you able to find an OD rain suit? I also could use a safety strap for my glasses.

Much love,

Peter

27 August 68

P.M.

Dear Mom, Dad, & Annette,

The rain suit arrived today. It's exactly what I needed and the fit is perfect. One word of caution however. The service personnel handling mail are pretty tough on packages. Yours arrived torn open completely on two long seams. So, I think you better tape and tie similar bundles in the future.

I still have not had the chance to buy a camera, and consequently feel I've missed some great shots. No sweat, I still have more time than I like to admit to take in Vietnam scenery with a camera.

Time really goes fast in the field. Since the duty day is 24 hours and there are no days off, the date or day of the week are meaningless and disregarded. Time is measured in terms of days one has left in Nam before coming back to the world.

The past few days, my platoon has been attached to an artillery battery for security purposes. This in essence, is like a vacation because the artillery sets up a position and waits for fire calls. Consequently, all we've been doing is sitting alongside of the artillery watching them rest.

The biggest benefit of this assignment is the chow. The artillery gets 3 hot meals a day. We've been trading the Arty boys our C-Rations for beer. The night routine is still the same – ambush patrols.

I would appreciate it if you could set up a subscription for me with the Record-Herald. I am getting tired of reading how great it is to be a soldier in Vietnam in the "Pacific Stars and Stripes" – when I can get hold of a copy.

Have Annette send me her new UW address before long so I can get her first impressions of being a Badger freshman.

Have you heard anything about the doings of Frank, I wrote him several weeks ago but haven't heard from him yet.

I'm trying to keep a diary of sorts because we've been doing a lot of interesting things and have had many unusual experiences. For example, on a sweep mission several days ago, two water buffalo downwind from me decided I didn't smell like a gook. They put down their heads and charged – I ran – but they ran faster – so I emptied a magazine in front of them at their feet. This changed their mind but an old papa san nearby looked mighty ticked off.

I really miss good eats like greasy, garlicky summer sausage. Another handy item is Kool Aid with sugar and Shake–a–Puddin'. Maybe you could remedy this situation for me?

Much Love,

Peter

"I can't see how I can keep my sanity
unless I lose my conscience and sense of justice."
– Peter Langlois

30 Aug 68
Friday – noon

Dear Mom, Dad and Annette,

Thanks for the glasses guard and the news clipping about [name withheld]. I will drop a line and tell him to head for Canada before he gets hung up with Sam's Vietnam tour.

Last night Alpha Company provided security for a company of ARVNs during a watch operation. If you think the U. S. Army is disorganized, you haven't seen anything until you've witnessed the ARVNs in action. They were all over the damn place. We never knew if the movement we saw was ARVN or VC. I'm surprised the two armies never fired at each other.

This screwed up junket lasted until 2:00 a.m. then we mounted our tracks and went out to the rural rice areas and set up along a road in a village as a blocking force for a sweep working our way.

The sweep approached us from the north – hence anyone coming to cross the road where we were from the north had to be kept on that side of the road until the Vietnamese security police checked their I.D. card. There was one hell of a lot of confusion – there always is when we have to handle civilians. Our one 13-year-old interpreter just could not move up and down a defensive line a mile long and effectively inform the people why they were being detained.

The CO's track was next to ours – this was our misfortune. He

Peter with Sanh, 13-year old interpreter

is very shallow and inept and has been relieved once of his former Vietnam command. At any rate, a mother with a baby in her arms explained to me she wanted to cross the road so she could go to her house (about 200 ft. away) to feed her child. Frankly on missions of this sort, "round up" is a better word, I feel as though I'm a storm trooper in Poland - at best, the neighborhood bully. To make a long story short, I let the lady cross the road – her husband and kids were calling to her from the other side. When the CO saw this, he blew his mind at both me and the mama san. He made me physically escort the lady back to her former place – she was hysterical and the baby was crying. I can't see how I can keep my sanity unless I lose my conscience and sense of justice. Such is the insanity of being in Vietnam.

The crowning blow was this. The CO had my squad set up a machine gun position on the road directly in front of a house. The gun was pointed right at the front door – about 50 ft. away. It was loaded, cocked and had a 100 round belt all set for action. At day break when the people living there woke up, they had a track with its 50-caliber machine gun pointed at them plus the machine gun I set up. I felt so low and ashamed that I could hardly look the villagers in the eye. After the run-in with the CO, the battalion commander came by and told me that I should unload the machine gun and aim it someplace besides the house because he didn't want the people to get a bad impression of us. Hell, the damage was already done, no thanks to the CO's lack of tact and compassion. Military logic stinks and especially here, does not fit the human factor into the equation for peace. What a paradox in a war when we must win the support of the people in order to gain peace.

Enclosed is a news photo from the "Stars and Stripes" [military newspaper] taken near Dau Tieng – our rear base camp. Notice the track in the picture. It's identical to the ones in the 2/22 Infantry. The one in the picture is from the 5th mech., who we'll be replacing soon in that area.

I've followed the political conventions on AFVN [Armed Forces Vietnam] radio. I think Nixon (my vote) has Happy Hubert beat before the campaign even starts. My vote is primarily against the administration's war policy – need I say more?

Much Love,

Peter

Top: ARVN, South Vietnamese soldiers; allies to U.S soldiers.

Bottom Left: Armored personnel Carriers (APC) also called "tracks". Peter, spent much of his year riding on or living in one of these tracks.

Bottom Right: M48 Series Patton Tank and villagers on bicycles.

3 September 1968 A.M.

Dear Mom, Dad, and Annette,

Yesterday I bought a camera at the Tan Son Nhut PX. It's a Japanese camera – 126C single lens reflex. The exposure is both automatic or manual and it has a mechanism on top for using flash cubes. Cost $49.50 – this would be $80-$100 in the U.S. The PX also has quite a selection of 35-mm's. If I had had the money, I would have bought a beautiful Yashica for $108. I'm sure that by the time I leave Vietnam I'll find a way to purchase it. Our ration cards only authorize the purchase of two cameras so the next will be the Yashica I described.

As I am writing, Alpha Company is set up out in the rice paddies as security for six 155mm Howitzers mounted on tracks. I've taken several pictures of the battery which should be interesting.

At the same time, people from nearby villages are milling about selling everything from cigarette lighters to "pot" and "boom-boom." It's more like a bazaar than a serious combat situation.

I hope the news photo I sent will give you some idea of the equipment used in a mechanized infantry outfit. One problem, the NVA base RPGs (an armor piercing rocket) raises total hell with track vehicles. An M-60 tank weighing 52 tons was blasted out of service by an RPG round several days ago near Dau Tieng.

We have a new platoon leader. He's a UW drop-out whose home is Madison. He went to OCS in the same battalion I was in and now he's in Vietnam as an officer. This new "leuy" is a career man and his "lifer" attitude has become a burden on the whole platoon. I think it will only be a matter of time before we can get him off his pedestal because so far, no one has been very responsive to him. This situation prevails because the platoon leader can't threaten any punishment. The worst thing that can happen to a G.I. now is having to serve a Vietnam tour with a line unit. Since this has already been arranged by Uncle Sam, each of us regards

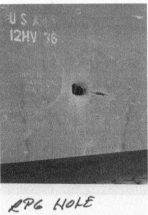

Top: Alpha Company heading out for an early morning sweep.

Bottom Left: Local villager selling to GIs.

Bottom Right: Damage from a rifle propelled grenade in the side of a "track." (Armored Personnel Carrier).

the man with the following attitude: "Either get with the program or get "screwed." So far he's been getting "screwed" for running a "loose ship" by our incompetent CO who seems to regress a little more each day. You don't have to look for humor in this company – the officers provide it free.

Reminder: Send me Annette's UW address.

Much love,

Peter

During his time in Vietnam, Peter moved up the ranks and was promoted to Specialist Fourth Class, Platoon leader, then by March 1969 he became a Sergeant with Company A, 2nd Battalion (Mechanized), 22nd Infantry. In a mechanized unit, soldiers patrolled the jungle with Armored Personnel Carriers (APCs) or "tracks" with weapons on board such as M-60 machine guns, an assortment of rifles, including M-16s and hand grenades.

— Annette Langlois Grunseth

*"As we moved down a narrow road leading
into dense foliage, the whole world suddenly
seemed to open fire on the tracks. To be exact,
the tracks were caught in an ambush."*
– Peter Langlois

1 October 1968

Dear Mom and Dad,

I realize that it has been some length of time since I last wrote; however, circumstances have been rather tense here. Consequently, there's been very little leisure time in which to write.

September 15, 2/22 infantry moved in convoy from Tan Son Nhut to division headquarters at Cu Chi. We spent three days pulling maintenance on the tracks, weapons, etc. and took on extra supplies, ammo and demolitions. Then September 18, the battalion moved again to an area out in the "boonies" northeast of Go Dau Hau. From our present logger site, Nui Ba Den, i.e., Black Virgin Mountain, is clearly visible. This landmark, you may recall from news reports, is very close to Tay Ninh – an area that is literally infested with VC and NVA.

We had to build bunkers and string rolls of concertina barbed wire around our new position. Filling sand bags for bunkers is especially tough work and the hot Vietnam sun is absolutely relentless. At best, this kind of work is nothing more than legal slavery.

September 19, we were still constructing our logger site when we received a mission. About 10 a.m. we moved to a large rubber plantation just north of Go Dau Hau in reaction to intelligence reports that alleged there was an unknown size, entrenched enemy force. At the edge of the rubber, everyone dismounted from the tracks except the driver, 50 cal. machine gunner, and the M-60 machine gunner. The dismounted troops started out on a long S&D (search and destroy) sweep while the tracks started moving through the rubber to form a blocking position on the opposite side.

The rubber plantation was very large and it took most of the afternoon for the tracks to move through it. I was on our squad's track as was the M-60 machine gunner. During this time the dismounted troops started to receive light fire from heavy cover along the edge of the rubber.

Late in the afternoon, the tracks broke through the far side of the rubber [plantation]. In the distance we could hear the volume of fire increase indicating that the ground troops now had made heavy contact.

As we moved down a narrow road leading into dense foliage, the whole world suddenly seemed to open fire on the tracks. To be exact, the tracks were caught in an ambush. The enemy had our position on the road zeroed in for mortars. The ambush was sprung by simultaneously firing mortars, RPG's (rifle propelled grenades), and heavy small arm and machine gun fire. One mortar landed in front of our track and another behind it. Bullets were ricocheting off the armor and cracking over our heads. Within seconds, our radio was crackling with screams of "medic, medic – I need a medic fast." Then,

"Hold your fire – don't shoot the fifties – you'll hit our own troops."

"For Christ sake get a medic, we've got a man bleeding to death."

"The sergeant is hit – his face is covered with blood. God, someone get the medic."

"We're receiving heavy fire – we need the fifties." "Hold your fire, pull back."

As we pulled back from the ambush kill zone, we opened fire with everything we had. The track ahead of us had taken a direct mortar hit on the fifty, spraying the gunner and driver with shrapnel. Back at the edge of the rubber, we formed a small tight perimeter. Everyone was still firing full volume as the bedlam continued.

The driver of my track jumped out of the driver's hatch and climbed on to the track that had been hit with the mortar. The fifty gunner was slouched over the remains of his gun. Our driver lifted him off the track and managed to get the wounded man behind the vehicle for cover. The gallantry was futile. The mortar had blown away a bicep, part of his head, and had made his chest crimson mush. As our driver laid the wounded gunner on the ground, his eyes rolled back and cast an icy white stare. He was dead.

The wounded driver managed to get off the track but he had to be led to cover because blood was running over his eyes. At this point, our element had 1 KIA and 3 WIAs.

One of the wounded was a sergeant who was shot through the side of his face. His eyes were bleeding and swollen shut. One cheek was a gapping red hole.

Our platoon sergeant started calling for a "dust off" but when the medevac chopper started to approach about 30 minutes later, it suddenly dropped out of the air from enemy fire. Another "dust off" made it in 40 minutes later.

It seemed like an eternity waiting for air support. Finally, gunships and several new Huey "Cobras" slammed machine gun and rocket fire into the enemy positions.

The dismounted troops were pinned down. While we waited for the dust-off, our platoon leader kept calling us on the radio, fearful he would get overrun. But we couldn't move until the wounded were taken care of.

Base Camp accommodations with sand bags

Just before dark, the tracks circled back through the rubber; crunched through several hedgerows and approached the pinned-down troops in a wood line across a clearing.

Once in the open, we opened fire, and roared into the edge of the woods. The whole area was a maze of red flashes in the dim light. Our superior fire power overwhelmed the enemy about an hour later. By now it was dark and we had to keep firing aerial flares so that everyone could find his way back to the tracks. Sniper fire continued and several enemy caught crawling in the light of the flares were quickly disposed.

At 8:30 p.m. we started driving back through the rubber. Choppers dropped flares for illumination. Back on the main road, casualties were totaled – 5 KIA and 15 wounded.

We finally got back to our battalion logger at 1:30 a.m. One track was left behind – blown apart in the ambush site.

Artillery pounded the scene of the fire fight all night and jets bombed it the next morning. Charlie Company swept the area in in expectation of a mortar attack on the battalion logger site. Everyone is tense and dog tired. The sun sets lower daily and torrents of rain make the landscape muddier every night. This is Viet Nam at present, a muddy, stinking hell.

Yesterday I was promoted to specialist four class. This means more money but it hardly compensates for the 24 hour - 7 day a week duty hours. Finally, I received your goody box, newspapers, etc. It was very much appreciated.

Much love,

Peter

the afternoon and found torn up bloody bunkers, a few weapons, but no bodies. The elusive enemy had disappeared with little indication of how badly he [the enemy] had been hurt.

Since the fight, we have found dozens of bunkers near Go Dau Hau and spent several days destroying them.

Each day we keep adding sandbags to our bunkers in anticipation of a mortar attack on the battalion logger site. Everyone is tense and dog tired. The sun burns daily and torrents of rain make the landscape muddier every night. This is Vietnam at present. A muddy, stinking hell.

Yesterday I was promoted to Specialist Fourth class. This means more money but it hardly compensates for the 24 hour – 7 day a week duty hours. Finally, I received your goody box, newspapers etc. It was very much appreciated.

Much love,

Peter

"Yesterday was by far the worst day of my life
and one I'll never forget."
– Peter Langlois

9 October 1968

Dear Mom and Dad,

You will recall in my last letter I mentioned that I had been promoted to Spec 4. The day after I wrote, my platoon leader moved me from track #23 (2nd platoon, 3rd squad) to be squad leader on track #22, the platoon command track.

Squad leader is normally a sergeant E-5's job, but due to a lack of NCO's, he had to use a lowly Spec. 4 like myself. I accepted the job on a temporary basis because the sergeant was in the hospital. Well, the usual squad leader was sent to Japan and now the platoon leader says he'll promote me to sergeant if I stay with the job.

Since I'm still trying to get the information job, I'm still acting squad leader and remaining non-committal.

As squad leader, the past week has been hell. The company moved to a logger outside Cu Chi along the highway to Long Binh. The second day we received a half dozen replacements and that night we were hit by an NVA ground attack. The trip flares in front of our position saved us because we got a jump on the gooks.

The big problem was to calm down the new men. Luckily, we had no causalities. However, we wounded an enemy officer and captured him along with an AK-47 rifle and a 60mm mortar tube.

Yesterday was by far the worst day of my life and one I'll never forget.

We had to sweep a road north of Cu Chi that led to an artillery fire support base. The engineers used mine sweepers but found nothing. It was terribly hot. I could only manage salt pills because food made me sick.

When we got to the fire support base, their equipment was being lifted out by helicopters. Our job was to secure a convoy of trucks carrying the excess of equipment the choppers couldn't handle. Personnel from the 101st Airborne stayed to secure the area.

As we pulled out, the base received mortar fire. Then, shortly, the lead track was blown up by a mine in the road we had just swept. We continued back to Cu Chi and dropped off the convoy and waited for them to unload. Then we secured the tracks again on the return trip back to the fire base to pick up the 101st.

Using the same road that had been mined, we moved slowly forward. Everything in the area was especially quiet. 23 track, my former squad, was ahead of 22 track as we started through a small village. At one point the road was covered with water.

As 23 forded this obstacle, it hit a mine and the guys I knew best and was closest to were thrown in the air and off the track into the mud. My senses were numb for about 10 seconds. Then I realized my buddies were hurt. Of the 8 men on the track, 5 had to be "dusted off" by Medevac Choppers. The squad leader had shrapnel in both arms and hands. Arteries had been severed and blood was spurting everywhere. He kept screaming, "Take care of my men" as the medics treated him. Another had a broken finger and shrapnel in his arms and face.

One of the other guys had a brain concussion and many shrapnel wounds in the face.

Another broke his leg when he hit the ground. The remaining guys were in shock but otherwise ok.

One man was still on the track – the driver. He was pinned in.

The mine had blown directly beneath the driver's hatch and torn a hole in the compartment. The bent, ripped metal had all but severed his left leg below the knee. Blood was gushing out the bottom of his compartment into the mire of water and oil the track was wallowing in.

The driver of my track and I dismounted and were the first to assist. 23's motor was still running and we feared an explosion. The blast had torn lose all the wiring around the master switch; the motor cover latch was jammed. The bare wire leads were shocking and burning the driver's leg. He kept screaming, "God help me, God help me." The engine was finally stopped when our platoon leader chopped off the battery cables in the rear of the vehicle.

At this point we started receiving light fire from both sides of the village but several tanks and gunships quelled it.

When the first "dust off" arrived, the driver [of 23 track] was still pinned. We sent back a request for a doctor and a cutting torch. In the meantime, a medic gave him morphine but he was still bleeding, screaming, and in great pain. We tried without success to free his hooked leg by reaching up through the hole in the bottom of his hatch. The leg felt like warm applesauce but couldn't be touched without him yelling all the louder.

When the doctor arrived, the driver had lost much blood and his breathing was getting short. The doctor had to amputate below the knee on the spot to save his life. He could only cut by feeling through the hole in the bottom of the track. The medic gave the driver two blood transfusions and a hypo but he was still conscious when the amputation started. About four minutes later he vomited and passed out. The crude operation took about 20 minutes and finally we were able to lift his limp body onto a litter and rush him to the chopper.

As the "dust off" left, I was aware of a peculiar smell about me. My hands and arms were covered with the driver's blood up to my elbows. I don't remember crying since I was a kid, but I had tears running through the mud and oil on my face at the end of the ordeal.

I went over to the remaining 3 members of 23 squad and tried to calm them down. All were in deep shock and covered with mud. At this point our interpreter brought in a VC they claimed had detonated the mine. He was blind folded and left in my charge. The damn "gook" kept moving around, and in a fit of emotional, animal-like rage, I grabbed him by the hair and threw him face down on the ground. He never so much as quivered.

Peter with AK-47 rifle recovered from the enemy. Note height and depth of sandbags behind him. Heavy work to fill, lift, and stack for protection.

The trucks we had been escorting made it to the fire support base and loaded the 101st personnel – about 30 to an open truck.

As we proceeded out of the area, the trucks were mortared – killing nine men.

I took a litter from our track forward to assist. The horror was beyond conception. Bodies were scattered over the road and ditch. One G.I. had his head blown off – another was crawling on the ground looking for his missing hand. All the while snipers impeded helping the wounded.

The enemy was almost god-like. He was everywhere and anticipated our every move. As we proceeded toward Cu Chi with the remains of our company, we were forced to shoot our way through another village – this time no casualties.

There are those who say God is dead but I'm sure they've never experienced the power of prayer as I did yesterday. I prayed for the men in my platoon and myself. We're still alive today. True, some are in pain, fatigued, nauseated or whatever, but we're still alive and that's all that matters.

I received your news clippings, letters, pictures and my Record-Herald subscription. You don't know how much it all means. Please keep it coming. Could you pay my alumni dues for me? All I have is military payment currency which I can't send. I'll reimburse you when I come home! Keep a record of it.

Much love,

Peter

P.S. I think this letter should be printed – perhaps it will get more people involved in the movement to end the war and madness of our involvement in Vietnam.

"There are those who say God is dead but I'm sure they've never experienced the power of prayer as I did yesterday. I prayed for the men in my platoon and myself."

"I don't remember crying since I was a kid, but I had tears running through the mud and oil on my face at the end of the ordeal."
– Peter Langlois

Pears

Growing up in the shadow of WWII my brother
grabs a pear from the Green Stamp fruit bowl,
pulls the stem out with his teeth, pretends to throw it,

making hand grenade blasting sounds.
He arranges green army men on the floor for attack and retreat,
plays war games in a foxhole dug into the empty lot next door.

As a Boy Scout he learns survival, camping out
on weekend bivouacs. With Dad, he hunts pheasant,
partridge, and sometimes deer. He becomes a good shot.

Like his father, uncle, and grandfather
he grows up to serve in the military.
His draft number comes up at college graduation, 1967.

After basic training, he flies off to Vietnam, barely prepared.
He writes home of government-issue weapons that jam,
they have no rain gear for monsoon season.

My parents buy a rain suit and mail it to him. His letters tell of
living in a "track" as they sweep the jungle, roll through
rice paddies, dodging snipers and ambushes.

Scouting and hunting skills keep him alive in that jungle.
His graphic letters detail how a bursting mortar
sprays a buddy's brains across his own helmet.

He tells me, *You have it easy*
because you're a girl,
you weren't forced into war, or that kind of fear.

Maybe I have it easier, but whenever I eat a pear
I feel his burden — my guilt ignites
as the taste of pear explodes in my mouth.

— Annette Langlois Grunseth

Music of Vietnam Part I

They connected to *I feel like I'm Fixin' to Die Rag*
and shout-sang *We Gotta Get out of This Place*
they were so ready to head to
The Green, Green Grass of Home

Where they dreamed of
Sittin' on the Dock of the Bay
after they mailed *The Letter*
from the land of *Purple Haze*

a *Fortunate Son* made it home
Leaving on a Jet Plane
maybe even for *Detroit City*
saving themselves, saving themselves.

— Annette Langlois Grunseth

October 15, 1968

Dear Peter,

Thanks for your last letter. Mom and Dad have told me about your letters too. It sounds just terrible and terrifying where you are.

It has been pretty wild here on campus with student protests. Most of the student riots are happening on University Avenue where my dorm room in Chadbourne Hall faces. I have a front row view as they throw bricks taking out windows of the campus Rennebohm drugstore. I can watch everything from my 5th floor window. Between protests if I need something, I dash over there to get my shampoo and lotion, then run back.

Each time the windows are broken at the drug store, a truck with large sheets of glass drives up to replace the windows. In a day or so the crowd is marching again with bricks, smashing those new windows. Plexiglass windows were installed next, those lasted a few days then a riot of students, police, and bricks took out those windows too. The windows have now been bricked up, walling in the drugstore. It's kind of weird going in there without any daylight, it feels like night even during the day, when inside.

Mostly I avoid the demonstrations, I don't want to get hurt. Everyone is so angry. The crowd spins out of control and I am not sure students know what they are even protesting. It feels like crowd mentality with uncontrolled anger. I hate the war too, but am not sure I see how violence is changing anything. Mom tells

View of University Ave. from Annette's fifth floor dorm window

me to stay out of it and not risk my life. I think she is exaggerating about it being life threatening. But still, I dislike violence so I stay out of it as much as I can.

How weird that we are both getting tear gassed! I am so afraid for you! Please keep writing when you have time.

We have a shared kitchen on each floor of the dorm so I will make some chocolate chip cookies to mail to you this weekend. (and yes, I will wrap each one in Saran wrap, like you asked).

Love, OOOXXX

Annette

Background of Campus Protests

Serious anti-war protests began the previous year on the University of Wisconsin campus in October, 1967 when students protested recruiters from DOW Chemical Company arriving on campus to interview graduating seniors for potential jobs. DOW Chemical made napalm, a flammable gel, that was used in Vietnam to burn large areas of trees and brush in order to discourage the enemy that was ambushing U.S. and South Vietnamese soldiers.

Anti-war sentiment continued on campus and when I arrived in the autumn of 1968, the first large demonstration was a week of protests against mandatory attendance by freshmen at the Reserve Officer Training Corps (ROTC) Orientation. Next, a mock cemetery was erected on Bascom Hill, the centerpiece of campus, to honor casualties in the Vietnam War. The "Milwaukee 14," a group that burned 10,000 draft cards of A-1 status came to campus to speak. Anti-war protests, as well as protests of other causes, continued for the next two years of my college life on the Madison campus.

Source: University of Wisconsin library archive, www.library.wisc.edu

Students, police and National Guard on the UW-Madison campus

Music of Vietnam Part II

Leaving on a Jet Plane

In Madison, I sway to the music of
Peter, Paul, and Mary at the Coliseum.
Leaving on a Jet Plane, a signature song for soldiers
captivates a thousand of us

spellbound by a three-hour concert.
We sing together in our youthful ideals –
peace, love, harmony, justice.
A generous concert with encores

and more encores, then they invite us to campus
for an all-night vigil. We sit with Peter, Paul,
and Mary in their aura, entranced
like cult followers, singing, crying

wondering where my brother and friends have gone
waiting for answers, only blowing in the wind.

— Annette Langlois Grunseth

""Every time I've been involved in a full-scale fire fight; every time I've seen someone collapse from wounds; every time I've seen a fellow G.I. die; I've prayed and asked for God's mercy for them as well as myself."
– Peter Langlois

*"The thought foremost in all our minds is thinking ahead
to the day a 'freedom bird' will fly us back to the world."*
– Peter Langlois

[letter written to friends and next-door neighbors]

30 October 1968

Dear Mr. and Mrs. H,

I would like to thank you for all the letters and interest you have taken in my welfare since I left home. Since my unit is in a rather remote area, mail delivery is sporadic at best. As yet I have not received the package you mentioned in your recent letters.

The McDonalds Hamburger franchise in Schofield has been sending me the Record Herald free. Consequently, I've had a chance to see my letters in print. Thought you might be interested to know that the editors have not deleted anything. Actually, I did not know my letters were being published until several had been printed and my parents sent the clippings.

You mentioned my letters were full of horror. All I'm trying to do is report things as I see them happen. God knows, I'm in a unit and area where just about anything is possible.

I suspect my letters might sound rather emotional and exaggerated. The emotional business is part of the fact that what I've seen is emotional as well as terrifying and nauseating. However, nothing has been exaggerated. I know it all must sound unreal but that's how it is in Vietnam.

Two nights ago about 7:00 P.M. our encampment received about 50 enemy mortar rounds. No one was killed but several dozen G.I.s had to be lifted out by Medevacs for shrapnel wounds.

Top to Bottom: Villagers travel a road with U.S. Army tracks nearby. Typical transportation of the local people.

The next night I was on an ambush patrol about 1,000 meters behind a village near our camp. Around 1:00 A.M. we spotted two VC moving on three sides of us but they never came close enough for us to spring the ambush. Last night another ambush patrol went back to the same spot. This time the VC walked right into the ambush. So far 6 bodies have been found and many blood trails. We're fearful now that the VC are caching arms for an attack on our camp. Earlier this week we found a complex tunnel and bunker system within 800 meters of our perimeter. We captured two POW's by throwing tear gas grenades in the tunnels.

81

The POWs have since pointed out VC amongst the civilian population – people who were working during the day for the Army inside our perimeter.

Tom mentioned he was interested in my opinion of the war. Well, here it is:

The U.S., I feel, has made a big mistake by accepting the major burden of the war. Our treaties with Asian countries commit us to aid, not save, countries that fall victim to Communist aggression. I feel more Vietnamese should be involved in major offensive action. So far the ARVN only assist the U.S. troops in this respect. In effect, we've upstaged the Vietnamese and taken over completely. If we pull out of Vietnam now, there would be a situation parallel to the Belgian withdrawal from the Congo a few years ago – chaos.

The armed forces make the mistake of not explaining to the servicemen why they are being sent to Vietnam and what we're trying to accomplish. This is not a declared war; we haven't been attacked on our own soil; and therefore, there is no great spirit of nationalism and positive popular support. Dissent at home has produced many people who doubt our intentions, as ambiguous as they may be, including many G.I.s. As a result, the most striking G.I. characteristic is his great apathy toward the whole Vietnamese "conflict." Command information is a total farce. When we leave our camp in the morning, no one except a few officers know what the mission is. NO one has made much of an attempt to encourage G.I.s to respect Vietnamese people, their customs, religion and mode of living in general. Every yellow slanted-eyed face is just simply regarded as another "god damn gook." The G.I., in short, finds it hard to sense any purpose for his presence in Vietnam and naturally loses pride in his work because little, if any, personal satisfaction is derived from it. A favorite G.I. phrase that is applied to just about any incident is: "The hell with it, it doesn't mean a damn thing."

Another great problem stems from a conflict between military, political and social goals. For example, an Army medical team will enter a village of illiterate rice farmers and establish rapport by offering much needed medical help. Next, the VC threaten the peoples' lives for cooperating with the Americans. Next, the military get wind of VC in the area. During the ensuing combat, the village and many civilian inhabitants are consumed. What have we accomplished? Nothing except instill hostility in the now suspicious and doubting villagers. In effect, it's a vicious, insane circle. We're trying to proliferate a paradox of conflicting goals. The military and civic minded leaders operate independently instead of cooperatively.

The thought most in all our minds is thinking ahead to the day a "freedom bird" will fly us back to the world.

Probably the best effect Vietnam has on any G.I. is that it makes one much more humble and appreciative of the United States and our way of life. At home we don't live in fear and suspicion of each other. There's no curfew, no hunger, no poverty, no widespread disease, graft, or illiteracy in the relative sense. Here all these factors are dominant elements in a way of life that, by U.S. standards, would not even be in existence.

I was very surprised to hear that Tom is now a school teacher. However, recalling his personality, I'm sure he can handle the job. I think he has the educational background and imagination to make his courses interesting and beneficial. At any rate, tell him I extend "rots of ruck."

Tom sent me the news clipping about Mack's fishing talents. How does it feel to be living with a local hero?

An edition of the Record Herald I received recently had some color photos of the Marathon County countryside in full autumn color. I've been suffering from pangs of homesickness ever since.

By now I imagine there have been some cold nights and frost. I'd give my right arm for some cool weather. The Vietnam winter

Infantryman, Peter Langlois, Dau Tieng

monsoon season with its deluges of rain has just ended. Now the opposite – the hot, dry season with its accompanying clouds of dust.

Many of our day missions involve providing security for supply convoys running between Cu Chi, Tay Ninh and Dau Tieng (near the Cambodian border), all on dirt roads. The route goes through endless miles of rubber plantations which are VC and NVA hiding places. The rubber has been cut back about 300 meters on both sides of the roads to discourage enemy attempts at setting up ambushes. Even these heavy security precautions don't prevent harassment – like mines in the roads, mortar and sniper fire. Being shot at is more or less part of the day's routine. Thankfully, the Reds are poor shots. Still, mines have blown up 8 of our "tracks" in the last month.

In closing, I would again like to thank you for your moral support. Your prayers are probably the most important and I hope I don't sound selfish in asking you to keep it up. I know something greater than all of us has kept me alive so far. Every time I've been involved in a full-scale fire fight; every time I've seen someone collapse from wounds; every time I've seen a fellow G.I. die; I've prayed and asked for God's mercy for them as well as myself. I know from experience "God is not dead." I'm positive he's been directly involved with me during some pretty tense experiences. A religious service over here really gives added meaning to being a Christian.

A chaplain wearing a steel helmet and flak jacket, preaching from an altar of ammo cans presents quite a vivid picture of "Onward Christian Soldiers." The lyrics of the hymn are much more meaningful when there's a choral background of artillery and gunship fire.

The chaplain cannot keep a regular schedule because the battalion commander won't let him into the area when there's heavy enemy activity and no one can be spared to provide security for him. In the meantime, individual prayer and faith provide some peace of mind.

I would enjoy hearing more local and neighborhood gossip – anything that doesn't pertain to death or fighting. I've seen enough to last a lifetime.

Yours very truly,

Peter

Mail Call

Everyone lived for letters. My brother wrote:
The only thing to look forward to in war is Mail Call,
Postage was free, a measly perk of war.

Everyone lived for letters.
We watched our mailboxes.
Soldiers had times to write and times to fight.

Mail traveled four days from Vietnam to Wisconsin.
Will there be a letter today?
Wally, our mailman watched, too.

When there was a letter from APO, San Francisco
addressed in my brother's large scrawl,
Wally rang the doorbell.

— Annette Langlois Grunseth

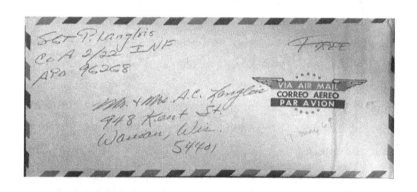

*"…we've had 13 straight days of enemy contact —
the first day was Nov. 1st — the day the
bombing halt was initiated."*
– Peter Langlois

"From the air, Vietnam is really quite picturesque.
The dark green rice paddies are divided into
neat symmetrical shapes by dikes."
– Peter Langlois

14 November 1968

Dear Mom and Dad,

I imagine you have been wondering about the effect the bombing halt and election have had on the combat situation in Vietnam.

I'm not asserting that there's any direct correlation but here's what has happened since November 1st.

On November 1st one of our tracks was securing a bridge site near Trang Bang. Late in the afternoon, a VC assassination squad approached the track from the rear in a small vehicle. At point blank range they jumped out of the vehicle and killed 3 or 4 men on the track. The driver, left for dead, drove the track back to Fire Support Base McNair where we were loggered. He had been shot in the head, stomach, and legs. I don't know how he managed to drive the track with such severe wounds.

To make matters worse, the VC stole an M-60 machine gun, four M-16s and a large quantity of ammo from the track.

Shortly thereafter, my company moved into an area south of Dau Tieng. It turned out to be extremely thick jungle full of thorny vines, insects, snakes, etc. This place is known as the Boi Loi Woods.

The Boi Loi Woods is very massive and its thick entanglement of vegetation provides perfect concealment for the VC. We made some RIFs (recon in force) by using our tracks to break down paths through the jungle but this turned out to be too slow to satisfy the battalion commander. He decided that airmobile op-

Tracks preparing to move into thick jungle of Boi Loi Woods

erations would be more effective. The irony of the matter is this: We're a mechanized infantry unit with no helicopter assault experience.

The battalion commander, therefore, decided we would become airmobile qualified by making chopper assaults in the Boi Loi Woods.

From the air, Vietnam is really quite picturesque. The dark green rice paddies are divided into neat symmetrical shapes by dikes. One sees herds of water buffalo grazing and tiny ox carts moving slowly between hamlets.

However, there is one major blemish that has all but ruined an otherwise beautiful view. Bomb and artillery craters pock mark the landscape. Only from the air, can one comprehend the destructiveness of our fire power.

The older craters contain water that is a beautiful aqua color.

It can be compared to the color of sea water in shallow coral reef areas.

The first airmobile assault we made turned out to be quite an educational experience. As the choppers circled the landing zone (LZ), air strikes and artillery prepped the area for our arrival. Then as we dropped toward our destination, the door gunners on the choppers opened fire with their M-60 machine guns. Just as we were about to land, more choppers came past us laying out a thick smoke screen to conceal us from the enemy if he happened to be near the LZ. The finale started as soon as we jumped from the choppers into waist deep water. Choppers firing rockets pounded the perimeter of the LZ for added security.

The LZ, as it turned out, bordered a deserted VC base camp, complete with a hospital and mess hall. The camp was under-ground-and completely camouflaged. Large bunkers with thick overhead cover were connected by a complex tunnel system. Our search turned up a large cache of rice, other foods stuffs, medical supplies, and clothes. We summarily burned everything, then put explosives in the bunkers and blew them apart.

On November 8th we made another air assault (eagle flight) into the Boi Loi Woods. About 3 p.m. our point element came under heavy machine gun fire. Word came back that the scout dog handler was dead along with an M-60 machine gunner. Our new CO, a former Park Falls [Wisconsin] resident, ran forward to assist. However, the VC were in well-hidden bunkers surrounded by heavy jungle foliage. As the captain ran toward the wounded men, the VC cut him apart from the waist down with a machine gun. Today his leg was amputated.

During this heavy fire, my platoon crawled toward the bunker. At a range of about 10 feet, my platoon leader had the magazine shot out of his M-16. Our medic, who was next to him, was not so lucky. He was killed by 3 shots in the forehead. The back of his head was completely torn off as the bullets made their exit.

Another man from my platoon was shot 3 times in the hand. Since then, his hand has been amputated. In all, 5 G.I.s were killed and 16 wounded. We quickly regrouped and set up local security while we waited for medevac choppers and an air strike. Both came and left. The air strike was impressive and noisy but completely off target. As soon as it was over, the VC hit us again – this time killing 6 and wounding 12 more G.I.s. The great frustration was that the entrenched enemy was devastating as well as invisible. The heavy cover concealed smoke and muzzle flashes.

Again, we called for air support however none was available except for the medevac ships. Our scheduled pick-up eagle flight wouldn't land to pick us up because the pick zone was too hot (under fire).

Our tracks had moved into the area but could not buck the jungle in the darkness. We buddied up walking through the jungle after dark to meet the tracks. Our movement was impeded by VC harassment fire all the way.

The tracks set up a perimeter in a small clearing for the night. We had no food or water until 10 p.m. when a chopper finally resupplied us. In the meantime, we had been digging in expecting the worst.

It came at 1:30 a.m. Mortars and RPGs (rifle propelled armor piercing grenades) rained in on us. One man was hit directly in the chest with an RPG, a weapon that can put a main battle tank out of commission with one round. His body from the waist up is still missing in action so to speak. Another G.I. was blinded by shrapnel that pierced his eyes.

This indirect fire was followed by a ground probe. We spent an hour peppering the wood line around our perimeter with 50 cal. machine guns and grenade launchers. As a last resort a napalm strike was called in followed by an air strike displaying 500 lb. bombs.

Sniper fire continued after the air strike. It was later quelled by artillery, mortars, and "Spooky" – a DC-3 with Gatling guns firing 6,000 rounds per minute. Needless to say, our perimeter has been smoldering ever since.

Daily RIFs in the area have uncovered 3 base camps containing hundreds of pounds of rice, mortar rounds, small arms ammo, and medical supplies. Still, the VC probe the perimeter every night. Nothing big, just harassment.

Everyone is exhausted. Resupply is so poor we've been eating one meal a day. The only thing that seems to matter to ranking officers is an enemy body count. In my estimation the new battalion commander must be crazed with his first taste of enemy blood. We have been given no support from other companies in this battalion. In effect, we're a little island unto ourselves in the middle of no-man's land. I've never seen more horror, blood, fear, and anxiety as I have here. So far, the bombing halt has not affected us positively – emphasize that we've had 13 straight days of enemy contact – the first day was Nov. 1st – the day the bombing halt was initiated.

I saved the best news til last. Today I was called in from the field to the company area in Dau Tieng. No reason was given. But, as it turns out, I'll be replacing the company clerk who will be going home soon. After the absolute horror of the past four months, I'm more than happy to be out of the field.

Even base camp living has its frustrations. The "hooch" I moved into this morning burned down this afternoon. Luckily, I was able to salvage most of my belongings. I lost some dirty fatigues and boots that should have been burned long ago anyway.

This brings things up to date. I hope you'll relax a little now that I'm a "chairborne ranger" in the company orderly room.

Much love,

Peter

From the Air

Helicopter blades whirl them up
in a swirl of dust; soldiers rising

into clean air, beyond the smell
of mortars, smoke, and death.

My brother sees green forests,
deltas, and rivers. He admires

the beautiful land, that in spite of war,
still has geometry of rice paddies

and farmers working with simple wooden plows,
creating quilts of crops below.

— Annette Langlois Grunseth

"My job necessitates that I identify bodies when G.I.s from our company are brought to grave registration after being killed in combat."
–Peter Langlois

23 November. 1968

Dear Annette,

I received your tapes. It sure was great to hear a familiar voice and the latest BS about the UW.

I still think it might be too early to determine whether or not music should be your major. If I were you, I would stick it out one more semester. But cover yourself with a few English courses if you can in case you make the switch. In the long run, English would be more beneficial unless you have definite career aspirations in music. However, ultimately the decision is yours. Make it early and avoid the last-minute rush to complete a major like I did.

Had a few laughs about your comments on your "gross" buddy at Chadbourne Hall. Meeting a variety of people, attitudes, and profanity are all part of the "sifting and winnowing" process at Wisconsin. It totally pissed me off that my four years went so fast. They're still the best years I've ever had.

I've had numerous letters and packages from my girlfriend. Seems as though she has the hots for me. Putting things in perspective, an R&R in Hawaii with my own personal guide might not be a bad idea.

Mom informed me that the November 13th Record Herald has one of my letters in it. If you've read the article you might be able to gather that we've been catching plenty of shit in Tay Ninh Province. Sparing the gore, I'll suffice it to say I've never known

Dau Tieng Base Camp

such fear, or seen more human waste. Vietnam simply sucks no matter how you look at it. Knock on wood for me - I'm lucky to be alive after all the crap we've been in since the famous bombing halt started.

Good News: Several days ago I was appointed company clerk at our rear area in Dau Tieng near Cambodia. So now I'm a base camp warrior. No more humping the boonies.

Still, it's impossible to get away from the presence of war. My job necessitates that I identify bodies when G.I.s from our company are brought to grave registration after being killed in combat.

My thoughts have been turning to Christmas. Bah Humbug. This is no place to be during the holidays. The hot dry season has begun and it just doesn't stimulate that Ho Ho feeling like it would be at home now.

Much love,

Peter

UW Campus Life

Greek was out.
Demonstrations were in.

Students weren't rushing
into Rush Week,

pledging was down,
fraternities and sororities dwindling.

Students pledged instead,
to march and protest.

Cheerleaders at Yell Like Hell,
pep rally at the Union for homecoming,

could not compete with
Hell No! We Won't Go.

— Annette Langlois Grunseth

5 December 1968

Dear Annette,

I feel like a real SOB wishing you a happy birthday a few days late. Don't get me wrong. I didn't forget. I've just been too damn busy to write anyone.

My new job as company clerk sounds like a real soft situation but believe me it's a real pain in the ass. I'm more of a babysitter for 182 people. However, it still beats humping the jungle and for once I feel like I'm doing something constructive in the Army.

How's by you the boy situation? Your letters and tapes sound discouraging but I know at UW there's plenty of studly type guys available. Maybe you're playing hard to get – hell, I don't know – the feminine mystique is Greek to me.

I just hope you don't get mixed up with some flower-power guy with beads and beard.

Has there been any talk about giving the football coach the douche? I've followed their record and it really sucks.

Dau Tieng RVN is very dry and dusty now as is most of the area. The 1st Cav. has a chopper pad next to the Company orderly room. When they land or take off, dust gets blown all over the place completely screwing up my beloved typewriter. No sweat, this is supposed to be a hardship tour anyway.

90-degree weather and dust just doesn't put me in the mood for Yippee Yuletide. Bah Humbug anyway. At any rate, hope your holiday season is merrier than mine.

Much Love,

Peter

Thanksgiving Break 1968

Homesick and finally home from college,
I join my friends at the local theater for a movie.
Any movie, just to be together. Gone with the Wind.

Civil War battles erupt across the screen,
rifles, pistols, cannons, smoke, dying soldiers,
heads and limbs blow across the screen.

Severed arms with limp fingers, legs in a wheel barrow
drip blood into the dirt as a medic disposes of amputations,
officials nail lists of the dead to the courthouse door.

Townspeople in the movie crowd to read the names.
They begin crying, screaming.
A hot lump grows in my throat.

Tears leak; I struggle for breath,
push back the lump — not now, not here.
I have no control. My heart races.

The curtain comes down, 20-minute intermission.

What if my brother doesn't come home? What if he dies?
The hot lump explodes into gushing sobs.
Friends have left their seats to buy candy and popcorn,

my best friend sits with me.
I rest my head on the seat in front of me.
She takes my hand, whispers, *He'll be ok.*

He will come home. He won't die. He won't die.
I hate this movie. It's only half over.
There will be more names of the dead,

cannons, blood, missing limbs.
I can barely breathe. Homesick
and finally home for Thanksgiving.

— Annette Langlois Grunseth

5 Dec 68

Dear Mom & Dad,

Your packages arrived completely intact. Everything you sent is just great. I couldn't ask for more. The brownies disappeared minutes after I opened the box. Slowly, I'm consuming the sheer volume of groceries.

The National Geographic Magazine with the article about the teenage sailor is outstanding. You used to hit the ceiling when I wanted to drive to Upper Michigan to ski. I guess the young sailor would have just about caused a heart attack if he had been me.

It has suddenly dawned on me that your whole mode of living must have changed quite a lot since Annette and I have both vacated 948 Kent St. What do you do for frustration and aggravation now?

Also, I'm curious about Annette. Has she sent you any bills for clothes? Knowing UW girls, she must have decided by now she needs a whole new wardrobe.

For once since I've been in the Army, I feel as though I'm doing something constructive. Actually, the job is a drag in one respect. I'm just a glorified babysitter solving the problems of 182 children.

No complaints though. There's been a lot of hostile activity in this area and Company A has been taking a good number of casualties both human and equipment. The only distasteful part of this job is identifying mutilated KIA's from the company when the dust offs come into Dau Tieng.

Several days ago, the VC zeroed in on the 1st. Cav. chopper pad next to our orderly room. The attack started at noon and only lasted about ten minutes. The first round sent shrapnel clanking off the metal roof of the orderly room. By the time the second one hit, we all had jumped into a bunker nearby. No one was hurt but several helicopters were pretty well riddled with jagged holes from shrapnel. That's about the most exciting thing that's happened since I left the Boi Loi Woods. I don't mind that at all.

Much Love,

Peter

5 Dec. 68

Dear Mom + Dad,
   Your packages arrived
completely in tact.
Everything you sent is
just great. I couldn't
ask for more. The
brownies disappeared
minutes after I opened
the box. Slowly, I'm
consuming the sheer
volume of groceries.
   The Nat'l Geographic
Magazine with the
article about the teenage
sailor is outstanding.
You used to hit the
ceiling when I wanted
to drive to Up Michigan

"Chairborne Ranger"
Dau Tieng, Vietnam

COMING IN FROM THE FIELD

JANUARY 1969

*"I was appointed company clerk at our rear area
in Dau Tieng near Cambodia. So now I'm a
base camp warrior."*
– Peter Langlois

5 January 1969

Dear Mom & Dad

I hope you had a good time during the holiday season. It's amazing just how little Christmas means over here. The dry season is in full swing and intense dry heat with unimaginable clouds of dust just don't provide for a "white" Christmas. I never realized it was Christmas Eve until I heard carols being played on AFVN radio. December 24th & 25th were the only days we heard any Christmas music. I suspect it was purposely programmed that way for psychological reasons and morale. In short, Christmas Vietnam 1968 was the same as any other day in this country – rotten.

The Bob Hope Troupe performed in Cu Chi on December 26th, however only 6 or 8 people from A company saw the show. These men were track drivers who had gone to Division ordinance to pick up new tracks to replace the ones that have been blown up by landmines in the roads around Dau Tieng.

I'm told that Hope's opening line was - "It's just great to be back at Cu Chi by the sea – the VC that is."

At 6 p.m. Christmas Eve the cease fire went into effect. There was no one firing or reconning by fire around the perimeter at Dau Tieng. The artillery batteries were ghost towns. No one was frantically yelling "fire mission" as usual throughout the night.

The mortar sections here usually fire harassment and interdictory fire at night along the edge of the rubber plantation surrounding the base camp. The familiar "thump" of mortars exiting the mortar tubes was absent.

Frankly, the silence made everyone, including myself nervous. This war is usually a constant, noisy affair but for 24 hours it was hard to imagine that someone in the nearby vicinity hated your presence. No one was fooled by the silence. Most of us spent Christmas Day in bunkers expecting the worst.

At precisely 6 p.m. Christmas Day the local artillery simulta-

Christmas
Dau Tieng
1968

neously fired about a dozen rounds from 8 inchers, 105mm how-itzers, and 175mm's. The VC returned the compliment with about 30 mortar and rocket rounds a few minutes later. Shortly the peo-ple manning the bunkers around the perimeter began exchanging fire with VC snipers in the nearby rubber trees.

At this point, everyone relaxed. We were back to normal, i.e. back to the war. That must sound like a sorry excuse for Christmas. It was and I'll never forget the holiday season 1968.

My job has developed into quite an educational experience. In essence I function as a crying towel, financial assistant, personal problems consultant, marriage counselor, and general vice president in charge of keeping 182 soldier-children happy in my spare time and try to keep up with the mound of paperwork that constantly smothers my desk.

The situation is made just a little more tense by the 1st Sergeant nicknamed "Deadeye." He must have been born with an incurable case of piles. No one can naturally be as ornery as he. He "bitches me out" instead of saying "good morning." He threatens everyone in base camp the he'll send us back to the field if we don't perform exactly as he decrees. However, I haven't had any trouble with him since I threatened to memorize some important documents and destroy them thus making me indispensable.

The company has a new CO. This is the fifth in 6 months. The first was relieved, the second wounded, the third relieved, the fourth wounded, and now the fifth. He's a West Pointer and just one hell of a decent person. The first four days he commanded the company, we killed 15 VC without any friendly casualties – a very unusual situation for this outfit. The morale has risen about 200% since he took over.

Here are a few examples of the problems I get confronted with. One of the men in the company wrote two letters, one to his wife and one to his brother. He absentmindedly put the letters in the wrong envelopes. His brother received some lovely text of love and assorted sweet nothings. His wife received an accurate grunt and groan description about the sex life of her husband with the local "boom-boom" girls.

The wife sent a letter describing the divorce proceedings she had initiated. So, this poor G.I. comes to me for advice realizing his classic mistake. I tried to look serious as I inwardly laughed my guts out. I told him to reenlist and make the army his new home for he obviously lost a happy one back in the world. This was said as a joke but damn if he didn't re-up for the "bennies" i.e. benefits, as they say.

My other problem child is a guy who has been in Vietnam for 7 months. He's been decorated for valor several times and was considered a valuable asset. Suddenly, he claims to be a conscientious objector and it's my job to help him prove he is one via applications, statements, life history, and various other trivia and assorted paperwork.

Everyone's got a problem or wants something. I feel like a vending machine that doesn't require money. What am I – a charitable organization? Everyone in this company seems to think so.

No sweat, I'm alive, no purple hearts, and I'm not humping the "boonies" with an M-16. That's compensation enough.

Happy New Year – Much Love,

Peter

P.S. Bought new SLR 35mm Yashica – Stateside $285. Vietnam price $140. More details next letter.

Company A
2nd Battalion (Mech.) 22nd Infantry
APO San Francisco 96268

5 Jan 69

Dear Mom & Dad,

I hope you had good times during the holiday season. It's amazing just how little Christmas means over here. The dry season is in full swing and intense dry heat with unimagineable clouds of dust just don't provide for a "White" Christmas. I never realized it was Christmas Eve until I heard carols being played on AFVN radio. December 24th + 25th were the only days we heard any Christmas music. I suspect it was purposely programmed that way for psychological reasons and morale. In short, Christmas Viet Nam 1968 was the same as any other day in this country — rotten.

8 January 1969

Dear Dad,

I am enclosing a check for $9.50. It's a refund from the outfit I bought a new 35mm camera from recently. Since there aren't any banking facilities closer than Saigon, you might as well keep the money as an additional payment on my bill for Alumni dues.

Today was a horror show. The 3rd platoon was ambushed in the Ben Cui rubber plantation just outside Dau Tieng. Three men were killed including a platoon leader and 11 men wounded. Two tracks were blown up beyond recognition.

I would make this letter longer and more informative except I'm in the process of gathering personal belongs and notifying the next of kin of the men killed and wounded.

I've taken pictures of the blown-up tracks – you won't believe the pictures. This bullshit about our control and superiority over here is the biggest farce going. The waste and loss of human lives and equipment is ridiculous. The military part of this war has got to become a 100% effort. The irony is that a medical team has just finished a big assistance program in the Ben Cui area. Three KIA and WIA were the reward. No one will ever be able to convince me that the U.S. is making much progress here.

Love,

Peter

Company A
2nd Battalion (Mech.) 22nd Infantry
APO San Francisco 96268

8 Jan 69

Dear Dad,

I am enclosing a check for $9.50. It's a refund from the outfit I bought a new 35mm camera from recently. Since there aren't any banking facilities closer than Saigon, you might as well keep the money as an additional payment on my bill for alumni dues.

Today was a horror show. The 3rd platoon was ambushed in the Ben Cui Rubber Plantation just outside Dau Tieng. Three men were killed including a platoon leader and 11 men wounded. Two tracks were blown up beyond recognition.

It Was to Die For

LBJ and McNamara
knew it wasn't winnable,
but kept sending soldiers to Vietnam
for another decade.
So many sons and daughters,
mothers and fathers
dead on both sides:
the innocent, the poor,
the uniformed,
the uninformed,
boots on the ground,
bullets in bone,
flesh on fire,
tirades of air raids,
glorification of body counts,
quantifying the unquantifiable.
How to measure a life?
How to end this tropical bloodbath?
War protestors crying, trying,
but the killing continues,
even death at Kent State.
Leaders hell-bent to save face
while soldiers had theirs blown off.
One soldier said,
It was to die for the biggest nothing.

— Annette Langlois Grunseth

January 1969

Dear Annette,

Most definitely congratulations are in order on your grade point average. I think this is a good indication that you have the UW under control.

The UW made the headlines recently in the Pacific Stars & Stripes. The story was titled "Bayonets on Campus." Sounds as though everything in Madison is normal.

Just out of curiosity, I'm wondering if you've involved yourself in any clubs, etc. The Hoofer sailing and ski clubs can really provide some good times and contact with people who share similar interest to yours. Besides, they're full of robust, athletic boys!

Many thanks for the goodies you sent. I'm completely amazed about the improvement in your cooking talents. The rest of the gluttons I live with agree.

As I'm writing, I'm in a bunker underground where I usually sleep. The TET holidays have started and the word is that 1 NVA division is supposed to hit Dau Tieng. Living in a bunker is just a precaution against the mortars and rockets that pop in here quite frequently.

As of March 1st, I'll be a sergeant. Seems the First Sergeant likes the way I've been mothering the "kids" in A Company. The longer I'm here, the more I'm convinced that the Army and this war are strictly a "mickey mouse" - "chicken shit" operation. God knows it's been an experience thus far. At any rate, I can't wait for my discharge and return to the USA in July. That will be the greatest birthday in 24 years.

Love,

Peter

Bayonets on Campus

In my brother's shadow at the same Big Ten school,
I begin freshman year, first time away from home.
The National Guard marches up Bascom Hill in formation,
they parade in unison like warriors, face shields
pulled down; rifles with bayonets propped on shoulders.

My brother sends letters from Vietnam.
He has an M-16, hand grenades, tear gas,
and describes surprise attacks on nighttime jungle sweeps.
Mortars crack over their heads in a ball of fire.
A land mine explodes underneath a tank.

He watches his buddy's legs get blown off.
Mother writes to me of the empty nest at home,
says the quiet is deafening. She cries
for her son's safety; she cries for my safety.
My brother writes, the headline of the

Pacific Stars and Stripes reads:
Bayonets on Campus in Madison.
As a recent grad, he jests, *That sounds about normal.*
I feel the burn of tear gas, fear guns on campus,
guards standing at attention outside my classroom door.

Police wield clubs against students.
I dodge canisters of tear gas lobbed at my dorm
as protestors run inside. I shake with fear
during riots on campus. I shake with fear
even more for my brother in Vietnam.

— Annette Langlois Grunseth

"The aftermath of any firefight is always the worst part of the enemy contact. The stench of bodies, the burning equipment and buildings, and the rancid smell of smoldering napalm is nauseating."
– Sgt. Peter Langlois

1 March 1969

Dear Mom & Dad,

I'm sure that by now you've heard about the new activity in Vietnam. Dau Tieng was hit just after midnight on the 23rd of February. Prior to the attack, things had been unusually quiet. The all too familiar daily mortar harassment and sniper fire was absent for about 2 weeks.

When the attack came, the "gooks" had obviously been storing up rockets and mortars for the occasion. Everything came in at once. The goriest "John Wayne" war movie ever made would have looked amateur after seeing this place lit up at night. The south end of Dau Tieng extends into a grove of rubber trees near Dau Tieng Village. This is where the attack came from.

Initially, a combination of rockets and mortars softened up this end of the camp. While the VC indirect fire kept us pinned down, the gooks infiltrated through tunnels dug from the village inside the perimeter bunker line. Everything was in chaos.

The enemy that got inside the basecamp was carrying satchel charges. Their main target was the maintenance area at the air strip where the spotter planes are kept. These aircraft are used to direct air strikes and to adjust artillery fire. They also carry rockets. The "bird dogs", as the spotter planes are called, are the best harassment we have "for Charlie." As soon as the pilot spots the enemy, he can direct the max on to the VC with air strikes and artillery.

The initial rocket attack had devastating effects. A rocket land-ed in an ammo dump near the spotter planes. Several cases of tear gas grenades were blown up forcing G.I.'s on nearby perimeter bunkers to evacuate the area. Without anyone to cover the fields of fire on these bunkers, the gooks had no trouble getting through the barbed wire. Which they did. An estimated two battalions tried to overrun the perimeter. Those that infiltrated blew up 4 spotter planes and a helicopter. A second objective was the fuel dump. The following morning 5 VC bodies were found next to it – all carrying explosives.

The major force in breaking up the attack was air support. Jets dropped napalm within 100 meters of the perimeter. This was fol-lowed by helicopter gunships firing rockets and machine guns. The sky was filled with smoke and bright red tracers all night. At about 9:00 a.m. the next morning the firing subsided, however, we were still finding snipers inside the camp at the end of the afternoon.

The aftermath of any firefight is always the worst part of the enemy contact. The stench of bodies, the burning equipment and buildings, and the rancid smell of smoldering napalm is nauseat-ing. The civilians in Dau Tieng Village were hysterical – the order went out to fire into the village when it became obvious that that was the source of the attack.

Our destructive capability has never been more apparent to me than it was in the village. At the same time the enemy proved again that he was determined and dedicated. However, many of the bodies had "pot" on them and the stench had a faint smell of marijuana. I'm sure anyone would not have tried what the VC did in a sober state of mind.

I can't help but think of what was gained by this attack. Both sides took heavy losses. 16 G.I.s were killed and 78 wounded. The enemy body count was at night – no one knows the real figure.

Bodies were piled up in the wire in front of the bunkers. In many cases just pieces of human remains were all that was left. One bunker that had been knocked out was covered with blood. In front of it were about 10 bodies and an assorted collection of limbs and flesh.

The next evening, we had another rocket attack. Ground probes continued all night, but on a minor scale. The hootch I was sleeping in has sandbags piled about 3 feet high all around it. At approximately 6:00 a.m. I heard a rocket coming in – it sounds like a big freight train bearing down on you. I started to roll off the cot onto the floor but I landed against the far wall. The rocket hit at the base of the sandbags – about 5 feet from my cot which was next to the wall. The shrapnel flew upward but the concussion blew me about 10 feet across the room. Luckily the only ill effects I suffered were shaky nerves. The wall above my cot was torn apart from shrapnel. How the debris missed me, I'll never know.

I'd sure like to know what the status of the peace talks is.

Dau Tieng is a scene out of a horror show. We've been on 100% alert since the 23rd of February – manning the bunkers every night. Each night a few more "gooks" [VC] are killed. You can't help but wonder when Charlie is going to get you. Personally, I think it's safer in the field. Here you're trapped within your own perimeter and can't maneuver around the enemy. Without air support, this place wouldn't survive another big attack.

Received a letter from Annette and the magazines you sent. I'm glad to hear Annette has adapted quickly to the UW. Her ideas and stories are all too familiar.

Much love,

Peter

Measures of War

Walter Cronkite, in our living room every night,
was the trusted face of reporting the war
with half a million boots on the ground in Vietnam.

Secretary of Defense McNamara,
former *Whiz Kid* of the auto industry,
now must measure progress of this war.
What can he count on to confirm success?

My brother writes letters home from the frontline.
He tells of combat, jungle sweeps, ambushes,
his buddies dying, grief pouring out like blood.
My brother asks, *Why are we here? What's the objective?*

McNamara measures bodies, like cars rolling off the line.
He counts enemy lives lost, says we are winning.
Walter reports of **our** soldiers lost, **our** dead,
and that's the way it is, night after night.

My brother writes of friends killed,
fears for his life, counts down the days.
Mother, a veteran, dizzy with distress of yet another war,
lost her brother in the last one. She lies awake at night,
worrying for her only son.

Secretary McNamara and President Johnson,
declare progress is being made;
my brother writes there is none,
Walter reports *the way it is.*

The common denominator is death,
where   every   body   counts.

— Annette Langlois Grunseth

March 5, 1969

Dear Peter,

I'm going to classes but some days it gets really hard. I was heading down University Avenue to my sociology class when a line of National Guard linked arms in front of the building where my class is held. One guardsman, in riot gear, shoved a club into my stomach yelling at me to leave. I told him I was just trying to go to class, and that I was not part of the demonstration. He didn't believe me so I had to leave and miss my class. That was scary for me, to get a club in the gut when I wasn't part of it at all.

The lobby of Chadbourne Hall was pepper gassed again yesterday. I came in from my afternoon class and could hardly breathe. I kept coughing and my eyes burned. I think the gas goes into the vents because we were still coughing in our room on fifth floor that night. This has been happening pretty often over the past couple of weeks. My roomie and I decided to move away from the action to the lakeshore dorms. We're moving out to Liz Waters soon. Most of the protests are in the southeast dorm area. I'm really tired of the riots and tear gas.

I have a philosophy class 8:50 a.m. Tuesday-Thursday. I was following a formation of guardsmen marching up Bascom Hill to go to class a couple days ago. When I went to my classroom on 2nd floor of Bascom Hall, there was a National Guard guy in riot gear, a clear face mask pulled down over his face, holding a gun with a bayonet, standing outside my classroom door! At least this time I could go to class. It's unnerving to have guards with GUNS outside each classroom in this building.

I hope you are staying safe. I wish you were on campus with me. It would be good to have some family here.

Love, your "little sis", OOOXXX

Annette

Police and National Guard stationed outside Bascom Hall, University of Wisconsin-Madison Feb. 1969

National Guard on duty outside classroom building.

[Peter's letter to next door neighbors, their oldest son, a close friend of Peter]

12 March 1969

Dear Mr. & Mrs. H,

I feel rather guilty writing to you so long after receiving your package. Hope you will understand that things have been very hectic here and also very tense. The NVA forces in this area have been putting the pinch on Dau Tieng with ground probes and daily, sporadic rockets and mortars.

The bunker where I sleep has been hit once, as well as our ammo dump. The NVA seem to have everything plotted well for their mortars. They've been extremely accurate in most cases.

Any time the company comes in from the field for a day or two, it seems to be standard procedure for our area to be mortared. Most of our hootches and buildings have frag holes and punctured roofs.

Time wise I will be a "2-digit midget" (less than 100 days left in Vietnam) very soon. It still seems like an eternity with all that's been happening here. My R & R – 10 April – will be a welcome treat. I had intended to go on R & R just before I came home, but decided I would probably have a nervous breakdown if I didn't take a break soon. So, April 4th I'm due to leave Saigon for Honolulu. It's a 12-hour flight with an hour stop in Guam.

I'm curious to know if you took a spring skiing vacation this year. The monotony of war, the Army, and Vietnam weather has bugged me to no end. The winter season and skiing are things I'll really appreciate the most when I get back to the "world."

I received letters from B.[Peter's friend, the neighbor's son, is a junior high school teacher].What has he been telling his kids about the war? Around Christmas-time his students sent me all kinds of greetings, which were very cute. Tell B. I appreciate their concern and interest. I'm sure his students must ask why we're involved in war. The best answer I think he could reply with is basically the major powers in this world haven't matured enough to realize the virtue of love and compassion.

I've sent several batches of pictures home, sent another bunch today. Hope you will be able to get some idea of what Dau Tieng is like. There are some gory war pictures taken shortly after the attack of 23 February. Those pictures are not the exception, but the rule. Results as they depict are common on both sides every day. These examples of depth in living color portray the futility of men who cannot compromise.

As you can see by my return address, I was promoted recently. At least as a sergeant, I don't have to put up with a lot of the trivia the Army thrives on.

Please give my regards to Bill, John and Dan. At this point I'm really counting the days until I leave Vietnam. People laugh about the slogan, "Wausau's Got it." I wish everyone had the chance to make the comparison I have for the last eight months. If anything, a year in Vietnam makes one a heck of a lot more appreciative of home.

Best regards,

Peter

Tropic Lightning News – March 1969 – (a Found Poem)

Uncle Gives Opportunities and Bennies During Your Viet Tour.
There is a job to be done in Vietnam.
Your career counselor would like to make you aware
of the benefits and opportunities available
during your tour here.

Have you thought about the additional money
you can make and save while in Vietnam?
All pay and allowances for enlisted men are tax-free.
You could receive an additional $8 to $22 a month,
foreign duty pay, tax-free.

Hostile-fire pay is an additional $65 a month, tax-free.
Free postage for letters home.
You get up to seven days of R&R for every 12 months of service.
For this R&R, the Army flies you free of charge to such locations
as Hong Kong, Bangkok, Tokyo, Singapore, Australia, and
Hawaii.

You may also go on a three-day pass within Vietnam.
As you can see, a tour in Vietnam offers
financial and career advantages.
Your career counselor has details
about this and other career opportunities.
He awaits your appointment in his office in Cu Chi.

— Annette Langlois Grunseth

(89 Days Left) Two-digit midget

18 April 1969

Dear Mom & Dad,

My R&R was simply fantastic. My female friend [from UW days] was a marvelous hostess and really went all out to show me a good time.

The plane left Saigon at 5 p.m. 4 Apr. 69 and stopped in Guam for refueling about 5 hours later. Anderson Air Base in Guam has a duty-free liquor store so during the 1-hour pit-stop, I bought a bottle of Chevas Regal Scotch and a bottle of Champagne for a total of $6.05! Thirteen hours after leaving Saigon, we landed in Honolulu, 12 p.m. 4 Apr 69.

Customs was a joke – we just walked through. Buses took us immediately to downtown Honolulu. Wives and friends of the people coming in from Vietnam were lined up on either side of a long hallway leading to the briefing auditorium.

Before I knew what happened, my female friend jumped out of the crowd, put leis around my neck and gave me a big kiss. What a welcome!

About ten minutes later, the Army turned us loose. The next six days were all too short, but simply terrific. My female friend has a car, an MG, so we were able to explore the whole island which is exactly what we did. We completely avoided all the tourists.

The first day she taught me how to body surf. In the process, I got smacked into the floor of the ocean several times and my female friend lost the bottom to her bikini in the surf. All in all, it was a fantastic day!

We went to a variety of wild places to eat and night club.

In most cases my female friend knew girls working in the night spots. This came in very handy because we were never charged full prices. (Took a cruise around Pearl Harbor).

The Hawaiian mountains are beautiful. We spent several days up in the rain forest.

121

The entire time a cool breeze was blowing and the temperature never got above 83-85 degrees. That was quite a relief from Vietnam. It was really depressing to leave.

We left Honolulu at 10 a.m. on the 10th, flew to Guam, then Saigon. Arrived in Saigon 6 p.m. on the 11th (90 degrees).

I received your post card from Florida and the news about the boat. If you compare Hawaii to Florida, I'm sure Hawaii would be more impressive – it's so casual. As I understand, the boat will be at Egg Harbor [Wisconsin] this summer. Sounds much better than the previous arrangement. What's the mileage from Wausau to Egg Harbor? Have you altered the engine problem in any way?

My return date is 16 Jul 69. I'll be going back to Oakland for separation processing. Anyone with 5 months or less left in the Army is automatically separated upon return to Oakland. This is the case with myself. I should be home as a CIVILIAN on or about my birthday.

The 11th Armored Cavalry is now working out of Dau Tieng. They have tracks plus tanks. It's nice to have the extra support inside this perimeter.

This damn place just continues to roast and blow dust around. Fortunately, the base camp hasn't received much hostile harassment recently.

The days are really dragging now that I'm getting short. Can't wait to see Wisconsin again.

Love,

Peter

P.S. Still waiting on the Record Herald with my pictures in it.

P.S. No weak moments on R&R, I'm still single, but very interested in altering the situation – but not too soon.

27 April 1969

Dear Mom & Dad,

I received the 7 Apr issue of the R-H [Record Herald] about a week ago. Everyone here who saw the full-page spread was highly impressed. I had many people ask for the issue, so to make everyone happy, I wrote a complimentary letter to Mr. Freund asking him to send about a dozen extra issues of the paper. Hopefully you saved a copy – I sent mine to my female friend.

Dad, how did you like Hawaii? Judging from the postcards you sent, you saw quite a lot of the smaller islands. I hope you were as impressed with Hawaii as I was. My guide was fantastic.

I'm still withdrawing from the effect of R&R. It's tremendously hard to leave the peace and fun in Hawaii and have to readapt to this bastard place.

Several days ago I was involved in the most tragic thing I've ever witnessed. At 1:30 a.m. 25 April, Dau Tieng came under a heavy mortar and rocket attack. Long ago, I learned that in order to survive in this place you must stay in a bunker after dark. Two very close buddies of mine, both top notch sergeants who were in Dau Tieng preparing to go home, elected to sleep in the tent adjoining my bunker. Both said it was too hot in the bunker to comfortably sleep.

During the first volley of mortars, a 120mm mortar came through the top of the tent and landed inside the tent at the edge of the entrance to my bunker. A 120mm mortar is approximately the same size as a small artillery shell.

One of the sergeants was sleeping on a cot with his head next to the bunker entrance. The other sergeant was about 10 feet away from his counterpart. I never heard the blast. I woke up choking – the bunker was full of smoke and debris. My left ear hurt like hell and my left leg had a number of stinging sensations. I tried to get out of the bunker twice, but more mortars and rockets kept landing in our area. The shrapnel was flying all over the tent.

I finally got out of the bunker after 2 more mortar barrages.

The sergeant who had been sleeping next to the bunker entrance was dead. The mortar exploded about 3 feet from his head. He was lying on the cot in the same position he fell asleep in. The top of his head was torn to shreds and his cot and the floor around it were a pool of blood. The other sergeant was still alive but unconscious. He died about an hour later from a deep sucking chest wound and from shrapnel in his throat and forehead. Most of his face was unrecognizable. When we lifted the dead sergeant onto a litter, his brains fell out of his skull onto the floor. Boris Karloff could never have dreamed up a more horrid scene. At the moment I can't sleep. Every time I close my eyes all I can see are the messed-up bodies of two GIs I knew very well. I should have learned by now it just doesn't pay to get very close to anyone over here. Death is so quick in Vietnam. There's no way to prepare for it.

About an hour later, it was brought to my attention that blood was coming down my leg. As it turned out, I had four small pieces of shrapnel in my left leg and a medium size chunk in the ass. The pieces in my leg were very small and easily removed. The one in my butt is still working its way out. The blast from the mortar broke my left eardrum. It's beginning to buzz and ding and the hearing is slowly coming back. The last several days, we've been repairing the bunker and cleaning up the atrocious smelly mess. It gives me the creeps to go near the bunker. The smell of death just hangs in it.

With only 80 days left in Vietnam, I'm getting pretty nervous after an experience such as I've just described. I try to stay near a bunker whenever possible. No one should be forced to live like a mole but that's exactly how I'm living now. God, this place is a nightmare.

Hope to make it,

Peter

WESTERN UNIO
TELEGRAM

THE SECRETARY OF THE ARMY HAS ASKED ME TO INFORM YOU THAT YOUR
SON, SERGEANT PETER R. LANGLOIS WAS SLIGHTLY WOUNDED IN UCTION
IN VIETNAM ON 25 APRIL 1969 BY FRAGMENTS WHILE IN BASE CAMP
WHEN THE AREA CAME UNDER ROCKET ATTACK BY A HOSTILE FORCE.
HE RECEIVED WOUNDS TO HIS LOWER EXTREMITIES. HE WAS TREATED
AND RETURNED TO DUTY. SINCE HE IS NOT REPEAT NOT SERIOUSLY
WOUNDED NO FURTHER REPORTS WILL BE FURNISHED

B-52 Airstrike, Dau Tieng

May 1, 1969

Dear Peter,

Sue and I have been settled in to Liz Waters for a month or so now. The lakeside of the dorm has patios facing Lake Mendota. Most of our classes have been cancelled due to the riots. One of my professors holds class at his apartment off campus - it's close enough for us to walk. The other professors cancelled classes.

I am taking Logic (a philosophy class), which counts toward the math requirement. I lucked out this semester because we don't have class very often and all the tests have been open book, take-home tests that we can do with other classmates. Several of us sit out on the patio of Liz Waters Hall, working on our take-home tests. We're all getting good grades so far.

This semester, I don't feel like I am getting my money's worth for tuition money spent. At least I am getting my credits toward graduation and living at Liz Waters has been good.

Mom and Dad flew me home for a weekend because they were so worried about my safety. There was a lot of violence, marching, and even tear gas going off near the lakeshore dorms.

Dad sent me an airline ticket, so all I had to do was get myself to the airport. I called a taxi for an early morning ride to the airport and the taxi refused to come on campus! I called another taxi service and finally one would come get me. The night before had been a really violent night, so when I came out of the dorm, I saw tear gas canisters littered all over the street by Liz Waters and the Sociology building next door. I could smell the canisters too. It looked and felt like a war zone.

Flying home was neat; seeing Madison from the sky. It was a rather short flight to Wausau. I spent a few days at home and read some of the letters you sent mom and dad. I am so worried for you! So glad to hear you were sent to a base camp now as company clerk. Stay safe.

I love you.....OOOXXX

Annette

Headlines from War

Shocking letters arrive at home
with tales of concealed tunnels
and Viet Cong ambushes

from everywhere and nowhere,
G.I.s are blown up like action figures.
Mother loses sleep, riveted to the news

she examines casualty counts
praying it won't be her son.
Life Magazine features faces of the dead,

yearbook-style, filling twelve pages in one issue.
Campus protests escalate as coffins arrive home
rolling across national TV.

Silent with worry, dad shares his son's letters
with the local paper. The letters are published,
it's one thing dad can do to help other families

who worry for their children away at war.
These parents call my parents
in mutual worry and support.

At the university I go to class,
avoid protests and police, stay out of harm's way
for my mother's sake.

— Annette Langlois Grunseth

Mother Writes a Letter to the President of the United States

[Our mother, lost her brother in World War II, missing in action over the pacific, his body was never found. She feared history would repeat itself with her son being killed. Here is a letter she wrote to President Nixon in 1969, which I found in one of her files after she passed away in 2011.]

May 2, 1969

The President
The White House
Washington, D.C.

Dear Mr. President,

I have composed many letters in my mind to the President of the United States during the past year, in complete frustration over the war in South Vietnam. Now I am actually writing this in desperation, trying to find some answers to very perplexing questions:

1) Why must the U.S. maintain military bases close to the Cambodian border that cannot be adequately defended?

2) Why cannot the U.S. blockade the ports of Haipjongg and Sihanoukville, at least, to prevent this constant flow of new troops and supplies from North Vietnam?

I know there are great risks and diplomatic problems involved, but the other risks are becoming more crucial as each day passes.

Our son, Peter, who is stationed at Dau Tieng with the 25th Infantry Division, has been sending us objective reports of the action there. He has not written his views on war strategy at all. In the midst of a horrible account of the latest ambush or rocket attack, he writes, " I wonder how the peace talks are coming along?" This question I cannot answer. I am enclosing a page from our local newspaper which is self-explanatory.

On April 27th, we received a telegram from the Secretary of

the Army's office saying that he had been wounded in the rocket and mortar attack on Dau Tieng on April 25th and had been returned to duty as he was not seriously wounded – thank God.

Yesterday his account of this attack came in the mail. His description is pure horror – the more tragic because his two buddies were killed. They were just about due to return to the U. S. Peter has 75 days of duty left and is wondering whether he will make it, as the base has been under almost constant attack for eleven weeks. They are living underground like moles.

Now we read newspaper and magazine reports, like this AP report in our Wausau Daily Record Herald, April 29, 1969: "Spokesmen said the bombing concentration in War Zone C is the heaviest of the war, with nearly 200 bombing raids flown along the Cambodian border in the past week."

The report continues, "The bulk of four North Vietnamese divisions is said to be concentrated in these two zones." (Earlier in this article they had referred to War Zone D, also). "For the past four years, U.S. troops have battled enemy soldiers in the 2,000 uninhabited square miles of War Zone C, but all the fighting apparently has resolved nothing."

"Two North Vietnamese divisions operating there have always been able to replace their losses from bases across the Cambodian border, using Zone C as a staging area for attacks into populated areas and allied bases to the southeast."

These AP reports have been amazingly accurate, they have corresponded with the information Peter has given me. My only conclusion can be this: Abandon the bases along the Cambodian border, unless we can go into Cambodia and attack the enemy that is constantly attacking our men. And/or blockade the ports supplying the North Vietnamese.

I know this is fraught with political and military dangers and that these suggestions are not at all new! However, I find it absolutely incomprehensible that any leader of any army of any country would expect these bases to survive under these conditions, let alone aid the military cause in South Vietnam.

This is not a reflection of any statements made by our son. He is too busy trying to stay alive to be able to philosophize about the war. It is his presence in War Zone C that forces me to write this letter.

I hope one of your secretaries will place this on your desk. I had to try to let you know my conclusions concerning War Zone C and in South Vietnam and can only hope it leads to a change in policy in these areas.

Thank you for the time it takes to read this (whoever reads it!) I pray that you will receive guidance from the God of Love in your formidable decisions.

Very Sincerely,

(Mrs.) Haldora B. Langlois

17 May 1969

Dear Mom and Dad,

Thanks for sending all the various publications. I really envy someone like the fellow in the National Geographic article who's so free to do something so "adventurous" as sailing around the world.

Dau Tieng and the surrounding exotic areas have been the victims of what appear to be a renewed offensive. The whole battalion has been in steady major contact the past four days. Dau Tieng itself is back to a mortaring and rocket schedule similar to Tet.

As a defense, myself and the others living in my bunker, have been adding extra layers of sand bags to the bunker. The four of us all have one thing in common – we're too "short" to take any chances.

I'm really laughing at your mention about the 25th Division returning to Hawaii, the same rumors have been circulating here but the rumor is being denied at higher-higher levels.

I hope there's a good run on the Carp River this year. From the way you've described the work load at the office, it sounds as though the fishing trip will be a well-deserved break for Dad.

What I'm really getting anxious about now is sailing. I'll really be curious to see the new arrangement in Egg Harbor. Are you getting a new boat or have the engine problems with "Naniboujou" been remedied?

How has Annette made out with her change in courses this Semester? I hope for the better.

The news about Grandy [Peter's grandfather] going to Oregon to fish really surprised me. I didn't realize he still felt so agile. I'm sure it will be good therapy for him after Mimi's death and playing "Mr. French" to the [other grandkids].

Mr. Freund sent the newspaper clippings I requested with my pictures in them. Let him know that I really appreciate his consideration.

Much Love,

Peter

[letter to the next-door neighbors]

17 May 1969

Dear Mr. and Mrs. H,

Thank you much for the package. Such gracious gestures are really appreciated. I really appreciate the mixed drinks. Alcohol is more or less taboo in Vietnam, so it's a treat to receive some in the mail.

Both you and my parents sound so terribly concerned about me being wounded. Please don't worry. It was nothing major and I'm all right now. Frankly, I guess I'm just exceptionally lucky. Close calls have been just a little too common for comfort.

My area in Binh Duong and Tay Ninh Province has been undergoing a renewed series of enemy offensives. Dau Tieng is back to a daily routine of incoming mortars and rockets similar to the Spring Tet aggression.

For the past four days, the 3 line companies in the 2/22 have been in firefights, all were major actions. At the moment there are about 20 men in the company who have been wounded who are recovering in the base camp. (20 men from A company). Another half dozen have been sent to Japan and are on their way back to the world. It's a miracle that only two men in A Company have been killed.

Rumors have been circulating that the 25th Division may be returned to the Schofield Barracks, Hawaii in about 60 days. It is still strictly a rumor – with 60 days left, it wouldn't do me much good anyway.

I regret I won't be able to see Tom and Mary soon. Their marriage always appeared to be assumed – I hope the draft does not interfere with their plans for VISTA. Advise Tom that he should start making tracks for Canada if he's drafted. This "conflict" in Vietnam is such politically controlled disorganized misery; it just isn't worth the added fear and tension for a newly married couple.

What is the latest progress with John Jr's movie making career? I wish I could be there to experiment with him. Since camera equipment is so cheap here, I've invested in a good 35mm camera and a telephoto lens. I'm looking forward to the welcome change of subject matter the U.S. will afford.

My best regards to you all and thank you again for the "care" package.

Yours Truly,

Peter

In June of 1969, near the end of my brother's tour of duty in Vietnam, *Life Magazine* published The Faces of the American Dead in Vietnam: One Week's Toll, which was laid out in yearbook-style showing names and photos of more than 200 soldiers killed in Vietnam during one week! I remember studying the photos and thinking that I was looking at someone who was now dead. I feared for my brother; would I ever see him again? We, the American people, were weary; this war was dragging on far too long. Was there progress? Were we winning? The Pentagon kept telling us that the United States was winning by tallying the number of Viet Cong killed every day, every week, every month. The war continued; soldiers died in combat for six more years.

— Annette Langlois Grunseth

*"Death is so quick in Vietnam.
There's no way to prepare for it."*
– Sgt. Peter Langlois

3 June 1969

Dear Mom & Dad,

Since I have not written for a long time, you're probably wondering how things are going in Dau Tieng. What can I say? It's extremely hot, more so than any other time while I've been here. We're all suffering from heat rash. Lately the rockets and mortars have been less frequent than usual. One can't deny the enemy's accuracy though.

About five nights ago, about 30 mortars landed in the artillery battery next door to us. This created secondary fires and explosions that blew up the artillery's ammo dump.

Eight inch and 175mm shells were popping off for four hours. We couldn't get out of our bunker because there was shrapnel flying all over the place. An incident such as this is more the norm than the exception in Dau Tieng.

The latest work (rumor) is that the Triple Deuce will be moving to Tay Ninh or Cu Chi. Supposedly, the 1st Division will move into Dau Tieng. The primary cog in the plans is the nature of Dau Tieng. No unit in the 1st Division wants our area – it's a booby-prize to whoever gets it.

Tay Ninh wouldn't be bad. I've been there before when we used to run convoys up there. Tay Ninh has had about 200 enemy rounds fired into it this year compared to about 1500 in Dau Tieng.

Cu Chi, Division Headquarters, is strictly for "lifers" and brass. It's too built-up and stateside like for me. Dau Tieng is a hot area but we are remote from all the "mickey mouse" that goes on in bigger base camps.

17 May our CO, his radio operator, and our Vietnamese interpreter were killed when one of them stepped on a booby-trapped artillery round. The CO was a great loss because he was such an outstanding leader and good friend to everyone in the company. The new CO is so indecisive that he scares everyone. He isn't half the man the former CO was.

Today I finally broke down and bought a stereo tape recorder.

Peter and other soldiers experienced severe sunburn and heat rash in the hot, humid climate of Vietnam.

It's a big Sony complete with speakers and built in amplifier. I mailed it home addressed to you. It should arrive in 3 or 4 weeks. Let me know when it gets to you and in what condition. Please go ahead and set it up. I'm anxious to know how it works.

Hope you're getting the boat all fixed up. I can't wait to go sailing next month.

Much love,

Peter

Extensive use of sandbags for bunkers and tents.

Sailing, Men on the Moon, One Digit Midget - July 1969

Dad steers the bow of the sloop into the wind.
Hand over hand I pull the halyard, raise the mainsail,
winch the last inches to the top of the mast.
Pushing the tiller starboard, dad turns the hull,
as wind gradually fills the sail.

He pulls in the mainsheet; we pick up speed.
I tug the starboard sheet to unfurl the Genoa jib.
The jenny billows as wind catches it.
I haul in the jib until it stops luffing.
Sails are trimmed in a close reach; heeling to starboard.

We sail past Welckers Point toward the lighthouse.
Gulls soar above the mast,
white caps chase down tops of the waves.
From the deck I stare at an azure sky,
think about the men who walked on the moon today.

It's almost my brother's 24th birthday;
he's a one-digit-midget in Vietnam
with less than five days until
he returns to the world.
I think about the men kicking up moon dust

and the napalm burning in Vietnam,
soldiers kicking up dust in combat
on the other side of our blue marble.
A sudden puff of wind catches the sails.
My brother said he misses sailing the most.

— Annette Langlois Grunseth

6 July 1969

Dear Mom and Dad,

The Triple Deuce moved to Tay Ninh about two weeks ago. Note the APO number change. The move itself was a real pain because so much equipment assigned to the company was unaccountable. At one point we were missing $26,000 worth of property. After much searching, checking serial numbers, etc., we located most of it. Then everything has to be packed and loaded on trucks. I felt there was a lot of indecision and confusion on the part of the leadership.

Our new area in Tay Ninh is very cramped and small. Worst of all, the previous unit in the area tore down their bunkers before they left. We are not allowed to build our own bunkers like we did in Dau Tieng. Here the engineers have to build them and we have not seen them lately. Tay Ninh doesn't receive incoming mortars like Dau Tieng did in frequent concentrations. However, they do get mortared and there's no place to go for protection at the moment.

Since our move, things have been very disorganized. "A" Company is working southwest of Cu Chi near Bao Trai, an open rice paddy area. "B" Company is working the roads between Dau Tieng and Tay Ninh. "C" Company is working the jungle north of Dau Tieng. In our case, we have been forced to establish a second rear area in Cu Chi for practical resupply. None of the companies in the battalion are working together which was very effective in the past.

June 29th to July 2nd, I had a 3-day pass to the in-country R&R Center in Vung Tao. Vung Tao is located on the coast north of Saigon. All the facilities are air-conditioned. The place is so beautiful it's hard to believe something like this exists in Vietnam.

I took quite a few pictures that I'm sure you will be interested to see. They're much different than the usual pictures I've sent home previously.

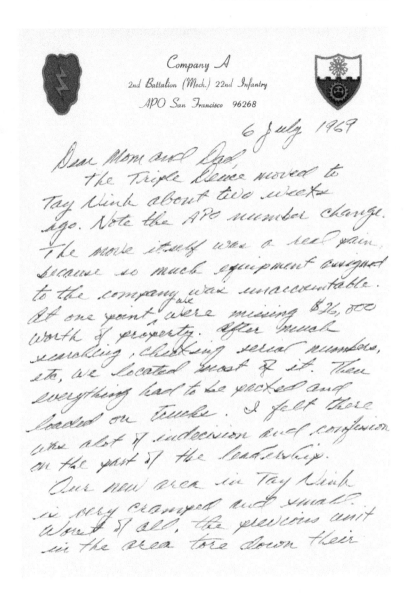

Company A
2nd Battalion (Mech.) 22nd Infantry
APO San Francisco 96268

6 July 1969

Dear Mom and Dad,

The Triple Deuce moved to Tay Ninh about two weeks ago. Note the APO number change. The move itself was a real pain, because so much equipment assigned to the company was unaccountable. At one point, we were missing $26,000 worth of property. After much searching, checking serial numbers, etc, we located most of it. Then everything had to be packed and loaded on trucks. I felt there was alot of indecision and confusion on the part of the leadership.

Our new area in Tay Ninh is very cramped and small. Worst of all, the previous unit in the area tore down their

Several days ago, I had to drive a truck from Tay Ninh to Cu Chi loaded with replacements and equipment for the company. I was really leery of running the road with only 13 days left in the Army. The route was along the roads that we have swept for mines ever since we've been in Tay Ninh Province. Not too far out of Tay Ninh, I noticed an ox cart moving slowly along the edge of the

139

road in the opposite direction of the convoy. As the truck in front of me went past the ox cart, the cart ran over a mine. The blast threw dirt up on the hood of my truck. The old papa san driving the cart went flying over the top of our truck and landed in the ditch. I doubt if he is still alive, he was pretty messed up. Although this is a very common occurrence in this area, it made me very nervous considering the time I have left.

The next day, I went out to the company field location with the resupply to see some of my close friends before leaving. The Bao Trai area is very similar to the Tan Son Nhut area - wet rice paddies, mud, and big marshes. The Company has gone the complete circle since I came to Vietnam. I don't envy the new men who will be sloshing around in all that water.

I'm glad to hear that my tape recorder arrived in working order. I was really concerned about it being damaged in the mail. Shortly, a large wooden box should be arriving at home. I would prefer if you did not open it until I get home. It contains some personal items along with various bits of junk I've acquired over here.

Dad's European trip sounds as though it was great fun. Uncle Sam's travel agency doesn't have any sense of humor at all in comparison.

Can't wait to see you all and get in some sailing time.

At the moment I'm the complete antithesis of everything military. I simply don't give a good Goddamn about Vietnam or Uncle Sam. In the process of the past 12 months I've busted my butt, stayed straight, and now I quit. I couldn't bear another day in the Army past 16 July.

I'm enclosing a copy of my orders just to prove my year in Vietnam is ending and my civilian life resuming.

Much love,

Peter

Takes Quickest Way Home

· · · Staff Photo

When a soldier heads homeward from the war he doesn't waste a minute getting there. Mr. and Mrs. A. C. Langlois, 948 Kent St., and daughter, Annette, were standing in front of Wausau Municipal Airport terminal Tuesday afternoon waiting for their son and brother, Sgt. Peter Langlois, to arrive on an Air Wisconsin plane. Peter walked out of the terminal to greet them. He had met his next - door neighbor, Robert Hertz, at a Chicago airport and accepted a lift home by car. He beat the airplane by two minutes. Peter, who served a year in the thick of it in Vietnam with the 25th Division and wrote a series for the Herald, left Saigon Sunday morning and had stops at Okinawa and Hawaii. Among his decoration is the Purple Heart for a wound he received as the result of enemy action.

Peter returns home!
Wausau-Merrill
Daily Record Herald
(name at that time)
July 1969

Chopsticks

You brought home gifts
from your tour of duty
as if from a pleasure trip,
a mini-camera for Dad,
a scarf for Mother,
and for me, chopsticks from Vietnam.
Two slender, black sticks the color of onyx
glistening in my hands,
each with inlays of pearly shell,
iridescent in marbled gold.
They made beautiful tools for eating —
people forced into famine,
their food defoliated by war.
You choked back that year of jungle sweeps
and body bags, all of it hard to stomach,
but you managed to forage a few gifts,
bringing me jeweled chopsticks,
tools of sustenance,
a souvenir of your survival.

— Annette Langlois Grunseth

A Second Chance to Live

A fox hole saved you in Vietnam
on that miserably hot, humid night.
You told us how your buddies
opted to sleep above ground
to escape the stifling heat in that bunker.

The mortar landed on top of them,
but the depth of that fox hole saved you,
the blast blowing you into the wall.
You came home. They didn't.

Partly deaf from ruptured ear drums,
and shrapnel peppered in your flesh.
You were given a second chance,
to marry, have children,
become a husband and dad,

to be a news reporter,
a public relations pro
for an insurance company,
and two paper companies.

It was a good second life
with family, some skiing, sailing,
a little camping thrown in.
It would've been happily ever after

except for buried anger,
your knotted silence, and
those cancer cells,
burning bright orange.

— Annette Langlois Grunseth

Part Three

"BACK TO THE WORLD"

Betty (Mother) Peter and
Al (Father) the day Peter
arrived home from Vietnam

Betty (Mother), Peter, Annette
(Sister)

Sniper in Vietnam

You tell about the VC sniper in the jungle.
You had your back turned.
Your buddy Larry sees him taking aim at you,
then picks him off with a clean shot.

After the war Larry visits.
Mother hugs him and cries
and cries, thanking him for saving your life.
I wonder, did the sniper have a home?
Did his mother cry too?

— Annette Langlois Grunseth

Not Welcome Home

Following discharge from the Army and a year in Vietnam-hell,
my brother was filled with sweat, nightmares, and shrapnel.
By luck and miracles, he made it *back to the world.* When he
returned to campus for grad school, his fraternity brothers'
hate-filled voices yelled *baby killer,* and *how could you go to
war?* Campus protests and demonstrations continued with the
National Guard close by.

Protesters with low draft numbers, would you have gone or fled?
Whose boots did you wear while protesting? Were they covered
in dust, mud, and blood? Did you hear the mortars whistling?
Were there snipers on your way to class? Protestors, couldn't you
tell the difference between the President's policy and a shocked
solider in a foxhole just trying to stay alive?

Hurling shouts and rocks,
students protest on campus.
Troops march up the hill.

— Annette Langlois Grunseth

Night Talks

After coming home from Vietnam, Peter enrolled in law school at the University of Wisconsin-Madison. When he returned to campus he was bullied as a veteran of war. He was called a "killer," as fellow students spit at him, and his watch was stolen from his room at the fraternity house where he lived.

Peter decided the UW campus was too hostile for him to continue school so he decided to leave Madison, returning to Wausau, not sure what was next. He landed a job in television news using his journalism degree. He monitored the local police scanners, dashing off in the TV station's news car with a cameraman at his side.

"Night Talks" after his last newscast of the day, 11 p.m. at home with the family cat.

Peter gathered news of the day, orchestrated the filming, edited his film at the station, and wrote news copy. He met deadline every afternoon, hitting the air at 6 and 10 p.m., Monday - Friday and often on weekends. He covered local, state, and national news, even reporting on the war from which he just returned. My brother told me years later this was his favorite job, saying he had control over the entire product from beginning to end. It was satisfying work that paid very little.

Since he could not afford rent for an apartment, he lived back at home for the time being. When he came in the front door after the 10 p.m. broadcast was finished, my night-owl mother was waiting up, having just finished watching him on the news. They would sit up late and talk, my mother resting at the end of the couch, feet up, an open newspaper spread cross her legs, under the glow of a pole lamp. After a long day at work Peter wilted into the high-backed chair, twirling a piece of his red-brown hair between thumb and forefinger, the family cat, Inky, curled up on his lap sleeping.

Over and over, he recounted the exploding track, the face blown off, the buddy looking for his missing hand, his commanding officer fatally hit. Mother and son talked of the senseless deaths, the unwinnable war, and politics in Washington until one or the other nodded off in the wee hours of the next morning.

Listening night after night, mother developed a nervous habit of rubbing the crown of her head with her middle finger. She scrubbed circles around that spot while he talked, scratching her head until a bald spot grew to the size of a quarter — her way to rub out his hurt.

— Annette Langlois Grunseth

Ongoing War

The Vietnam conflict, (really, a war)
was over in 1975, but never over for you,
a thousand secrets held within.

Flashbacks, like an immoral movie, played in your sleep.
A nonstop nosebleed prompted tests;
your blood work was off the charts.

For fifteen years cancer cells tunneled
like a search and destroy mission,
sweeping the delta of your thickening blood.

Scraps of Agent Orange
hid and divided inside you,
your jungle of sick, thick.

T-cells mutated,
and the brain was seized
as cells multiplied and misfired.

Your memory and motor function
grew tangled, then tumbled.
Doctors were puzzled about this invasion.
A casualty of living; your war raged on.

— Annette Langlois Grunseth

Invisible Wounds

Sutured in silence
he stopped telling the stories,
got on with life, family, a job.
Kept the blood and mess of war
out of his house.

But what he saw in Vietnam
could not be un-seen.
Stitched into his soul
was the worst day of his life
and another,
and another,
too much death, gore, grief.

Anything might trigger his temper:
his boss at work,
cold eggs served at a restaurant,
potato salad served on a bare plate
without *even a god-damned lettuce leaf* for garnish.

Years later when hostages
from the Middle East were released,
arriving home, praised, cheered on TV,
his anger burst open
Where was my welcome
when I came home?

He raged about being
spat upon, taunted,
when protestors shouted
How could you go to war?
How many did you kill?
Nothing was left unsaid.

Nothing could be undone;
He unraveled from
the shunning and shaming,
a most unwelcome home,
his wounds no longer
sutured in silence.

— Annette Langlois Grunseth

Post-Traumatic Stress

As the years passed, I asked, "Peter, your letters are really well-written, did you ever think of publishing a book?"

My brother was silent. He changed the subject.

More time went by; our mother would echo, "Your letters are good, they need to be published."

He did not reply.

Peter loved autumn, especially the brilliant reds, yellows, and oranges of the leaves, the deep blue skies and frosty fall air in northern Wisconsin. Our two families would return to our hometown in north-central Wisconsin to enjoy hiking in the woods, raking leaves for our parents, and having a good visit where the cousins could play together. One autumn visit, I nudged him again about publishing his letters.

More silence.

When he first came home from Vietnam in late July 1969, he told me, "One day I was in Vietnam getting on a plane to fly 'back to the world' and 24 hours later, boom! Here I am in Wisconsin; it was a shock, a complete culture shock. Everything in Nam was so very different from here. They have nothing; we have so much. They barely eke out a living farming. Our stores are jammed with food, clothes, and anything we want."

He continued, "We received little debriefing to prepare us for coming home. I just grabbed my duffel bag, and got the hell out of there with my discharge papers in hand."

After the first couple of days he was home, our family was in the backyard on a July evening. He spread out large topographic maps across the green lawn showing us the areas in Vietnam where he fought in the jungle. He told stories until long after dark.

Peter mailed home rolls of film during his year in Vietnam. My parents had the film developed and photos printed as the rolls of film arrived. When he came home, a stack of envelopes was waiting for him. He sorted through the photos compiling an album that essentially illustrated the letters he sent home.

I found the album difficult to look at, and years later I was told that my brother rarely looked at it. After Peter had passed away, Mother kept asking me about the album and feared it was lost. I promised her I would keep trying to find it. The album remained stored in the bottom drawer of Peter's file cabinet which is where I found it a decade after his death.

Over the years, I have read and reread his letters. Since my parents kept the letters in their safe deposit box, and Peter lived in Minnesota, and then Iowa, I doubt he ever reread them. His wife and children knew little about the letters or the photo album.

I was told Peter experienced nightmares and woke up one time in a sweat, yelling out, with his hands around his wife's throat -- he was dreaming that he was choking a Viet Cong! Death filled his dreams. His terrifying experiences were buried deep within.

Sometimes he would talk about the putrid smells and the dust of Vietnam. He said, "You never forget the smells." I tried to imagine, but could not. He said, "Decaying flesh was the worst of all. You never get the smell of death out of your head."

Those times when we were together, if he heard a helicopter flying, he could identify a specific "chopper" just by hearing the type of "thwap, thwap" of the blades in the sky, even off in the distance.

Hearing fireworks popping and booming in the air, he said, "They sound just like the night flack we would get." He told me never to surprise or startle him because he might just go into "attack" mode.

In the early 1980s my parents and Peter's wife, recognized he was struggling. Was it depression? Anxiety? It didn't have a name yet but his wife took him to a psychiatrist in a nearby city, seeking help, hoping for answers. Peter saw it as a personal weakness and not his fault, blamed the doctors, and refused help. Much later, we learned it was undiagnosed post-traumatic stress (PTS).

He didn't talk much about what happened in Vietnam, but one evening his wife told me that he blew up at the TV, yelling in anger when he saw soldiers returning from the Middle East as they were being honored with parades and cheers. He was bitter and angry about not being welcomed home.

During the 1990s we were both at the peak of our careers, and raising children. After my workday I put in a "second day" at home, fixing meals, helping our two children with homework, doing laundry, then sneaking into the kids' rooms in the dark to put their clothes away, hoping not wake them. I was lucky if I could fall into bed by 10:30 p.m. I would just be drifting off to sleep when the phone would ring about 10:45, which was when Peter wanted to talk. He'd tell me about his day, struggles with his boss, current projects, and whatever else was on his mind. I was exhausted but I listened. It would be 11:30 p.m. or close to midnight when we'd hang up.

During Peter's funeral visitation I heard similar stories from his closest friends; they too received those phone calls, always after 10:30 p.m. We had to laugh that we were part of Peter's "exclusive" club of late-night phone calls.

I cannot begin to know the burden he carried for 35 years after Vietnam. He made it back alive, but was changed from the person he used to be. I feel a great deal of sorrow for the trauma he experienced and a certain amount of guilt that I had an easier life than he had, mostly for being female and exempt from the draft.

I grieve for Peter, who lived with physical and emotional pain, eventually succumbing to a war-related illness. Now I am glad he did not revisit his own letters in vivid detail – it would have been too painful; but half a century after the Vietnam War, it is time to give voice to his story.

Reflection
(after the painting, "The Wall" by Lee Teter)

His temples pound,
hand pressed to the black marble,
heartbeat pulsing his hand.

He hears the fwap, fwap, fwap
of chopper blades —
the enemy surging like ants, from their tunnels.

He feels them drop out of the jungle.
Bullets streak from everywhere and nowhere.
Gunfire slices the night.

Sweating and inhaling the humid jungle
he says you never forget the smells.
Innocent looking mama-san carries

grenades tied up in her hair.
He shuts them all out,
the choppers, the wounded cries,

the red mush that was once a leg.
He slowly blinks, traces names of buddies,
touches their memory

on this marble bunker,
catches his breath and inhales
the April fragrance of cherry blossoms.

— Annette Langlois Grunseth

A Rare Cancer

Peter not only experienced emotional trauma from the war, but also at age 45, developed a rare cancer related to Agent Orange exposure.

Agent Orange was a concentrated combination of chemicals sprayed liberally to defoliate the Vietnam landscape, exposing the enemy, and destroying crops and the food source for Viet Cong as well as civilians. The high concentrations of Agent Orange may have achieved its objective for war, but in the decades since, there have been serious consequences that would affect large numbers of Vietnamese and U.S. soldiers.

Peter experienced sudden, gushing nosebleeds, fatigue and other symptoms. Preliminary bloodwork showed strong abnormalities in his blood cells. Peter was eventually diagnosed at the Mayo Clinic in Rochester, Minnesota, with Waldenstrom macroglobulinemia a very rare cancer, especially for someone in their forties.

Waldenstrom macroglobulinemia caused his bone marrow to produce too many abnormal white blood cells that crowded out healthy blood cells. The abnormal blood cells produced a protein that accumulated in the blood and impaired circulation. It is a type of non-Hodgkin's lymphoma on the slow growing spectrum of cancer. It is not curable and is usually found in much older adults.

Mayo Clinic specialists were perplexed as Peter's illness was their first case of a young person having this illness. His treatment plan was their first for a person his age. Peter lived with Waldenstrom macroglobulinemia for 14 years, going to an outpatient clinic for chemotherapy. He told me that a couple times a year he also went to the cancer center to have his blood stripped of the extra protein. He explained a process where his blood was routed through a machine to be "cleansed" and then returned to his body. Peter would say, "It's time for me to get my oil changed again." He managed to keep a sense of humor in spite of the seriousness of his illness. A decade and a half of outpatient chemo infusions and oral chemo eventually wore down his body. The last two years were a slow decline of complications from ongoing chemo, and eventually his brain was affected. It was agonizing for all of us in the family to watch him go through these treatments, exploratory surgery at one point, and constant appointments that lead to a steady decline.

This Agent Orange related cancer and its complications ended my brother's life when he was only 59 years old, on December 18, 2004.

— Annette Langlois Grunseth

His Last Summer

He sought solace in the woods,
the cool lake air,

loons calling to each other,
a woodpecker drilling in the distance,

fish nibbling circles on the water.
We had a week together up north

shortly after his 59th birthday.
There was a tremor in his hands and his voice.

I don't think I am going to have a very long life,
he said, watching the sun drop into the lake.

— Annette Langlois Grunseth

Mothers Still Worry, You Know [3]

Mothers still worry about their little boys, you know
He's not doing well, my brother's wife says
My eighty-four-year-old mother needs to see her first-born
We drive from Wisconsin to Minnesota to Iowa

He's not doing well, my brother's wife says
as we follow black pavement slick with rain
We drive from Wisconsin, to Minnesota, to Iowa
My brother's wife says, *Only 59, he looks like an old man now*

as we follow black pavement, slick with rain
We arrive in time for dinner, shocked at his decline
My brother's wife says, *Only 59, he looks like an old man now*
Mother sits next to him, her blue-veined hand holds his

We arrive in time for dinner, shocked at his decline
His hand quivers, eyes look flat with a gaze of giving up
Mother sits next to him, her blue-veined hand holds his. She says,
Mothers still worry about their little boys, you know

— Annette Langlois Grunseth

Coming Home Again
For Peter 1945-2004

Coma is the comma
before crossing over,
a sad parting
for those of us left behind.

For you, no more nightmares,
no more flashbacks,
or the stinking heat
you hated.

No more slow drip of chemo,
no more probing brain surgery,
no more shaking behind a walker,
IVs removed.

You've come home again
to the cocoon of a hospital bed
in your own living room, a week before Christmas.
You turn your head to see the decorated tree.

With no words left in you, your wife whispers,
You're home for Christmas!
You gently slip into a twilight coma.
Sheeba, the cat, snuggles in the curve of your

fetal-curled legs; she never leaves your side.
You didn't make it to Christmas, or maybe you did,
traveling your last R & R.

— Annette Langlois Grunseth

Once Hot, Forever Cold

I

In Vietnam my fair-skinned brother
suffered heat rash, blistered lips, sunburn,
nicknamed "red" by his Black buddies.
He endured stifling nights, sun-scorched days

while the politics of war heated up at home.
Soldiers lived by the calendar
crossing off the days,
one by one, for staying alive.

II

Stunned to survive
he came home to excess,
unrest, searing contrasts of culture.
He pieced together a singed soul.

His short fuse shot off
like a geyser at irregular intervals,
trauma and stress simmered and seethed,
then cancer ambushed him.

A fifteen-year struggle for a cure
that was not to happen,
his body withered, shut down,
gave out.

III

His funeral two days before Christmas,
dawns with an arctic blast, iced streets,
twenty-two below zero.
In honor, we walk behind the hearse

from chapel, to church, to cemetery,
our frigid feet sting as we walk,
breath thick as fog around us,
huddled in coats and cortege.

We grieve at the grave,
flinch as guns fire a military tribute,
the flag from his casket is folded,
as hot tears burn our iced cheeks.

— Annette Langlois Grunseth

Part Four

WHEN WILL WE EVER LEARN?

Resemblance

Years after my brother's death,
I visit his family in Iowa.
Friends from their church exclaim,
We see Peter in your face,
haunting, yet comforting.

As brother and sister,
we share same fair, sandy hair,
same smile, same Chicklet teeth.
Am I the ghost of my brother,
come back to remind them of what they lost?

I'm the little sister who wasn't drafted into war
now haunted by the extreme luck I was dealt.
I miss him too; our shared DNA lives on.
Combing my hair, I catch a glimpse
of his teasing smile in the mirror.

— Annette Langlois Grunseth

Irony of it All

Returning from Vietnam
my brother saw no flags waving,
heard no cheers,
only jeers, and stares,
when they spit insult on injury.

The 60s
hatred of soldier and sacrifice.
Anti-war. Anti-service.
Anti-anything established,
no pomp under this circumstance.

The 70s, 80s, 90s
life moved on
while remnants of war
soured his soul,
no accolades until decades later.

Too little, too late, he said.

The irony of it all
when agent orange
and cancer consumed him,
mourners lined up for hours
to view his body.

Three days and three nights
of prayer and pomp,
flag-draped casket,
military medallion on his granite stone.
Welcome Home, Brother.

— Annette Langlois Grunseth

At the Ike Sturm Jazz Ensemble Concert

A soft jazzy voice begins,
croons like clouds floating on light,

*The autumn leaves
        drift by my window*

*the autumn leaves of
        long ago.*

A vibraphone velvets the air;
saxophone spirals its notes around us.

The heart-pulsing rhythms of
drums and string bass snare my thoughts.

Are there even words for
what I feel billowing inside?

Vibraphone steals a melody from the vocalist;
sax runs away with it.

A montage of music rushes over the audience,
then tones break apart on separate paths.

I follow one of the melodic trails.
It takes me back to my brother who loved jazz

and jazz-cool autumn in the forest,
kicking up a rhythm of leaves fallen from

maples *turned red and gold,*
like the words warbling now.

I wander his woods with these words,
gather in the colors of music and leaves.

Come, follow the jazz trail,
let go and listen —

I miss you most of all,
when autumn leaves start to fall.

— Annette Langlois Grunseth

My Mother's Moon

Her day was not complete
until she stepped out to see the moon.
It might be an orange ball rising,
or a white turtle egg hovering.
More than a thousand full moons
shadowed my mother.
She studied the moon when Neil Armstrong stepped upon it.
She cried for her son who saw the same moon rising
over rice paddies and incoming mortars in Vietnam.
There was the empty nest moon the autumn I left for college,
but the loneliest moon was the August my Dad died.
The moon of selling her house changed the view,
rising to different walls. Yet it was always her moon at bedtime.
She loved the strawberry moon, harvest moon,
eclipses of the moon, the Indian summer moon.
And finally, a full moon rising on her last night,
crickets in the grass singing.
I held her hand, bed pulled close to the window,
moonlight falling gently across her face.

—Annette Langlois Grunseth

The Inheritance

WWI,
My grandfather lands on
French shores at 23, fresh out of
dental school, serving his country,
fixing teeth, trained in healing, not war.

WWII,
My grandfather's son
flies reconnaissance over Japanese shores
tucked in the nose of a B-29,
shooting photos not enemies.

Valentine's Day 1945 military police knock
at my grandparents' door. They learn their only son
is missing-in-action. Oh! The years of pain, not knowing,
always hoping he might walk in the door.

Vietnam
Granddad, your first-born grandson flies to Vietnam.
You fight back tears; he fights back Viet Cong.
He survives snipers, ambushes, tunnels, and attacks.
He comes home filled with anger and Agent Orange.

1981
Dear Granddad, today I birthed your first great-grandchild.
I hug Crisco-slick newborn, warm on my tummy —
feel a chill.
It's a boy.

— Annette Langlois Grunseth

The Bottom Line[4]

Not far from boyhood he was sent to war,
deployed to a valley in the shadow of death –
chaos in the jungle, the agony it bore,
the blood, dust, and smells stole his breath.
Viet Cong attacked from tunnels underground
in the chaos of ambush he was ordered to kill.
Snipers in the trees fired hundreds of rounds,
both sides were shooting when his buddy went still.
Death was so quick, it shocked right to his core,
when he came back home, that scene flooded back,
nightmares of trauma bled deep grief and gore.
He was never the same, still living the attack
then cancer from war seized him cell by cell,
dying, he asked – *Do soldiers go to hell?*

— Annette Langlois Grunseth

Making Peace

Peter made it "back to the world," earning a Bronze Star and Purple Heart. Like so many veterans of war, he rarely spoke about the horror he saw in Vietnam. He came home a changed person, with a more serious demeanor. The nightmares, flashbacks, pain, and anger of post-traumatic stress from combat stayed with Peter for all thirty-five years after returning home.

He continued in journalism with a first job in television reporting, even covering news about the war from which he just returned. Through the years, he worked in several corporate positions in public relations and marketing. He was an outgoing, people-person in his career, and yet underneath, he had much weighing on his heart which he kept hidden, as did so many Vietnam veterans.

In his last fifteen years of life, he grew spiritually when his wife introduced him to an orthodox church in Iowa where they lived. Church members embraced him, he met other Vietnam Vets there, and also served on the parish counsel. The priest teased that he should get a "feather in his cap" for transitioning from Unitarianism to Orthodoxy. He joined a special group of prayer brothers who shared their Vietnam experiences. They carried each other in support. Peter asked for forgiveness for the atrocities of war, confessed, and felt relieved to be forgiven for all that had happened.

He was grateful to have made a life and had a family following the war. His wife, Anne Marie, shared that she never knew the extreme depth of his sorrow until the family visited the Vietnam Veterans Memorial in Washington DC in October 1998. Peter sobbed and broke down at the wall, touching the names as he made rubbings of three brothers he cared about deeply: Commanding Officer, Capt. David R. Crocker, Jr., Sgt. John E. Bladek, and SSgt. Michael R. Dorman. He regarded these men as competent, brave, and compassionate.

Peter loved the outdoors with skiing, hunting, fishing, and boating. As a final salute for his soul, two months before he passed away, he took a solo road trip to Mitchell, South Dakota, to Cabela's sporting goods store, a touchstone of joy for active outdoorspeople. He went there to try on Carhartt jeans, even though he "knew." Peter returned without the pants, but gifted his wife with an orange-red raincoat.

After that, he declined rapidly, spending a month in the hospital, then was brought home to a hospital bed in the living room a couple weeks before Christmas. The articulate journalist, now unable to communicate, spoke with his eyes at the sight of the Christmas tree.

There is no place on the Vietnam Veterans Memorial wall in Washington D.C. for veterans like Peter who survive the war and succumb to its effects years later. On behalf of my family, we honor and remember the life of Peter R. Langlois, brother, husband, and father – may his memory be eternal.

— Annette Langlois Grunseth

"On Behalf of a Grateful Nation..."

one for my grandfather
one for my uncle
one for my brother
one for my mother
one for my dad

tightly folded into
thirteen triangles
fabric snapped
folded in precision
hand over hand

stars for our states
face outward
stripes of the original thirteen
concealed inside

white gloved hands extended
on behalf
of a grateful nation...
never heard what was next

emotion overtaking
the undertaken
thanked for
their service
their sacrifice

constellations
confined
inside isosceles
of glass and oak
three cornered
shadow boxed
each grief contained

— Annette Langlois Grunseth

GLOSSARY OF ABBREVIATIONS AND TERMS

AIT: Advanced Infantry Training (next level of training after Basic Training)

AFB: Air Force Base

APC: Armored Personnel Carrier, also called "tracks."

APO: Army Post Office is associated with Army or Air Force installations. Mail to my brother in Vietnam would go through an Army Post Office (APO) in San Francisco, before it shipped out to Vietnam.

AFVN: Armed Forces Vietnam. Refers to the Armed Forces Vietnam Radio station.

ARVN: Army Republic of North Vietnam, Vietnamese soldiers on our side during the war; U.S. soldiers were helping to train.

BCT: Basic Combat Training

Bivouac: A temporary camp without tents or cover for the purpose of training soldiers.

Boom Boom: "Boom-Boom" girls were local Vietnamese women who were prostitutes during the Vietnam war. Soldiers also referred to having sex as getting some "boom boom."

Chairborne Ranger: Soldiers in administrative duties.

Charlie: In Vietnam, it was a term for the enemy. 'Viet Cong' was abbreviated to V.C., which in the military phonetic alphabet is 'Victor Charles,' which was shortened to 'Charlie.'

Civies: Civilian clothes

CO: Commanding Officer

CONUS: Continental United States

Dustoff: It was difficult to rescue wounded soldiers in the thick jungles of Vietnam, and often roads were blocked from landmine explosions. Using helicopter ambulances was an efficient and fast method to fly in, pick up wounded soldiers and transport them to medical treatment quickly.

"In April of 1962, the 57th Medical Detachment (Helicopter Ambulance) arrived in Vietnam with five UH-1 "Huey" helicopters. They took the call sign "Dustoff." Over time the number of medevac detachments grew in Vietnam until the entire country had coverage and "Dustoff" became the universal call sign for all medevac missions. A "Dustoff" crew consisted of four people: two pilots, a medic and a crew chief."

Peter Langlois wrote "dust off" as two words in his letters.
Source: www.vietnam.ttu.edu/resources/dustoff/

Genoa jib – A sailing/nautical term for a large staysail that extends past the mast and so overlaps the main sail when viewed from the side, nicknamed a "jenny." – *Wikipedia*

G.I.: Government Issue, also refers to soldiers being government property.

Gook: An insulting and derogatory slang term for Vietnamese, Korean, and Southeast Asian people. It was used by U.S. soldiers during the Korean War, and more extensively during the Vietnam war. U.S. soldiers might have heard locals saying "miguk," the native word used to name the country of America, and then was misinterpreted by soldiers who thought locals said "me gook."

Happy Hubert: Mentioned in one of the letters, "Happy Hubert" was a nickname for then Vice President of the United States (1965-69) Hubert Humphrey from Minnesota, who was the Democratic nominee running against Richard Nixon in the 1968 Presidential election.

Hootch/Hooch: A hut or simple dwelling, either military or civilian. Peter lived in a hootch while in base camp.

I.G.: Inspector General

KIA: Killed in action

"Logger" site: As mentioned in the letters, being "loggered" and "logger site" is a defense perimeter, often a wire, fenced in area of protection for soldiers to retreat to from the field. The actual spelling is lager, but in the jargon of the Vietnam War soldiers spelled it "logger."

MOS: U.S. Army alpha-numeric code to identify a soldier's Military Occupational Specialty. MOS is the job in which the G.I. was schooled and trained to perform.

Source: http://ed-thelen.org/MOS-Vietnam-era.html

Peter referenced MOS in his 10 May 1968 letter from Ft. Benning, Georgia, while in training.

Mechanized: Mechanized infantry means with armored personnel carriers (APCs) or infantry fighting vehicles (IFVs) for transport and combat. Mechanized infantry is distinguished from motorized infantry in that its vehicles provide a degree of protection from hostile fire by having weapons on board.

NCO: Non-Commissioned Officer, often a platoon leader or staff sergeant. In Vietnam when a commissioned officer was killed, a non-commissioned officer who demonstrated leadership qualities might be assigned to step in to lead a unit. A non-commissioned officer has risen through the ranks and been promoted for excellence in performance. A non-commissioned officer has not received a formal commission such as from a military academy, officer candidate school or other military program.

NVN: North Vietnam

OCS: Officer Candidate School; extra training to become an officer.

OC: Referred to in the letters is short for Office Candidate.

OD: Olive Drab, the basic U.S. Army color.

PX: Post exchange. A military shopping center where soldiers can buy items at a discount.

Reds: "The Reds" refers to the Communists or North Vietnamese soldiers.

RIF: Reconnaissance (recon) in force. A heavy reconnaissance patrol that goes out ahead to scout out possible traps and ambushes.

RPG: Rifle propelled grenade, aka armor-piercing rocket.

RVN: Republic of Vietnam

R & R: Rest and Relaxation, a weeklong break from a war zone in a safer place.

Sheets: A sailing/nautical term that refers to all lines (ropes) on a boat which are used to control the in and out motion of the sail – *from the Common Sailing Glossary of Terms.*

SOP: Standard operating procedure

Triple Deuce: Refers to the 2nd Battalion (Mechanized), 22nd Infantry Regiment.

Tropic Lightning: The patch of the 25th infantry, was called Tropic Lightning, also nicknamed the "Electric Strawberry" it was their logo or symbol for the division, with which soldiers identified.

VC: Viet Cong, Vietnamese Communist. North Vietnam sympathizers and/or enemy citizen soldiers in the south who might be employed by the U.S. government by day and fight against the U.S. at night.

VISTA: AmericCorps VISTA. A federal agency for community service and volunteerism.

WIA: Wounded in action

The World: Soldiers in Vietnam referred to home in the United States as "the world." As in, coming back to "the world."

Sgt. Peter R. Langlois graduated from the University of Wisconsin-Madison in 1967 with a bachelor's degree in journalism and advertising. He earned his master of science degree in administrative studies in 1997 from the University of South Dakota.

He enlisted in the U.S. Army and served in Vietnam with the 25th Division. He was awarded the Bronze Star and Purple Heart medals.

After the military, he returned to Wisconsin to work in journalism, public relations and marketing. He was a news reporter/news anchor with WAOW-TV, Wausau, Wisconsin. He worked in public relations and advertising for Wausau Insurance Companies in Wausau, Weyerhaeuser Company in Wausau, and Blandin Paper Company of Grand Rapids, Minnesota. He moved to Iowa to continue his career with MidAmerican Energy Company, where he worked from 1983-1997. He then worked for Morningside College and the American Cancer Society of Sioux City, Iowa. He was an avid outdoorsman and enjoyed hunting, fishing, boating, and skiing. He passed away from an Agent Orange related cancer in 2004.

Annette Langlois Grunseth, author of *Becoming Trans-Parent: One Family's Journey of Gender Transition,* (Finishing Line Press) was nominated for a Pushcart Prize and has published widely in journals and anthologies such as *Midwest Prairie Review, Wisconsin People and Ideas, Dispatches Magazine* (Military Writers Society of America), *No More Can Fit Into the Evening* (international anthology 2020); *The Ariel Anthology, Portage Magazine, Walt Whitman Poets to Come,* (bicentennial anthology), *Soundings: Door County in Poetry,* and *Halfway to the North Pole,* among others. She is a longtime member of the Wisconsin Fellowship of Poets (WFOP) while also being recognized for her poetry with WFOP and the Wisconsin Academy of Sciences, Arts and Letters (University of Wisconsin).

After a career in healthcare marketing and public relations, Grunseth has focused on writing poetry and honoring her brother by publishing his letters from Vietnam. She lives in Green Bay, Wisconsin, with her husband, a disabled Vietnam Veteran, where they enjoy the outdoors and advocate for human rights.

Website: **www.annettegrunseth.com**
Facebook, LinkedIn, Instagram, Twitter
Contact: **annettegrunseth@gmail.com**

RESOURCES

Veterans Administration www.va.gov

Veterans Suicide Prevention Hotline www.veteranscrisisline.net/

Alpha Company, 2/22Infantry: www.vietnamtripledeuce.org and www.2ndinfantry.org

END NOTES:

[1] July 1965: President Johnson calls for 50,000 more ground troops to be sent to Vietnam, increasing the draft to 35,000 each month.
Source: https://www.history.com/topics/vietnam-war/vietnam-war-timeline

[2] On January 23, 1968, the USS Pueblo, a Navy intelligence vessel, is engaged in a routine surveillance of the North Korean coast when it is intercepted by North Korean patrol boats. According to U.S. reports, the Pueblo was in international waters almost 16 miles from shore, but the North Koreans turned their guns on the lightly armed vessel and demanded its surrender. The Americans attempted to escape, and the North Koreans opened fire, wounding the commander and two others. With capture inevitable, the Americans stalled for time, destroying the classified information aboard while taking further fire. Several more crew members were wounded.
Source: https://www.history.com/this-day-in-history/uss-pueblo-captured

[3] The poem "Mothers Still Worry, You Know" is a pantoum.

[4] The poem, "The Bottom Line" is a 14-line sonnet.